The Illustrated
WISE WORDS & COUNTRY WAYS

Sarah

with love & happy
memories of a special weekend.

Ruth

The Illustrated
WISE WORDS &
COUNTRY WAYS

RUTH BINNEY

D&C
David and Charles

In memory of my parents who, by nature and nurture,
gave me an enquiring mind.

A DAVID & CHARLES BOOK
David & Charles is a subsidiary of F+W (UK) Ltd.,
an F+W Publications Inc. company

First published in the UK in 2004 as *Wise Words and Country Ways*
This illustrated edition published in the UK in 2007

Reprinted 2008 (twice)

'Never Smile at a Crocodile' (p 226) words by Jack Lawrence, music by Frank Churchill,
© 1952 Walt Disney Music Company

Distributed in North America
by F+W Publications, Inc.
4700 East Galbraith Road
Cincinnati, OH 45236
1-800-289-0963

A catalogue record for this book is available from the British Library.

ISBN-13: 978-0-7153-2776-0 paperback
ISBN-10: 0-7153-2776-3 paperback

Printed in Great Britain by CPI Antony Rowe.
for David & Charles
Brunel House, Newton Abbot, Devon

Commissioning Editor: Neil Baber
Editor: Emily Pitcher
Assistant Editor: Sarah Wedlake
Project Editor: Beverley Jollands
Designer: Eleanor Stafford
Production Controller: Beverley Richardson

Visit our website at www.davidandcharles.co.uk

David & Charles books are available from all good bookshops;
alternatively you can contact our Orderline on (0)1626 334555
or write to us at FREEPOST EX2 110, D&C Direct, Newton Abbot, TQ12 4ZZ
(no stamp required UK mainland).

CONTENTS

INTRODUCTION

Every year on 22 December – the day after the winter solstice – I would sit at breakfast, waiting for my father, a physics teacher, to open his paper, look at the date and declare that 'As the days lengthen the cold strengthens'. So began my interest in old sayings and in science. If we were out together on a winter's night he would look for a ring round the moon as a sign of 'snow soon' and he often related how, as a child of the Edwardian era, he would be given on his birthday a maxim to follow for the year ahead such as 'Do your duty like a soldier and a man'.

The sayings in this book, collected in the years since my childhood (when we were allowed to have our hair washed only once a week and schools gave girls prizes for good deportment), relate closely to the business of everyday life, largely as it was lived before the days of modern conveniences, and how they relate to modern life and knowledge. They include advice on the practical necessities of cooking, gardening, keeping house and health, as well as proverbial wisdom concerning good behaviour for children, adults, and life in general.

Many of the old adages our grandparents believed in have since been proved true, though others, like putting butter on a burn, have been discredited. But it is probably no accident that many once-valuable items such as salt, eggs and silver recur in the old sayings or that they have much to say about foretelling the weather. For in the days when most people made their living from the land, being in tune with nature could be vital to survival.

For the superstitious, there are dozens of old country sayings and traditions that relate to good luck, good health and finding a spouse, as well as to omens of disease, death and disaster. Almost everything was once invested with significance, from seeing a single magpie to the day of the week on which you did your washing or cut your nails.

In compiling this book I have used numerous sources old and new, but have drawn particularly on the 19th century classic advice book *Enquire Within*, a bound-up collection of the magazine *Home Chat* from 1896, *The Concise Household Encyclopedia* of 1933 (discovered at our village fête) and, from the USA, *The House and Home Practical Book*, also from 1896. I have not, however, tested the old recipes included in the book, so they are used at your own risk.

My thanks are due to the team at David & Charles for believing in and refining the book concept, and for preparing this illustrated version of the original, to RoSPA and the RSPB for supplying essential facts and to friends who have lent books and imparted information of all kinds. Special thanks go to my daughter Laura and to my husband Donald, not only for reading the manuscript but for spending many hours at secondhand bookshops and stalls at home and in Boston and New York, helping me to unearth those invaluable nuggets of reference that have brought this book to life.

Ruth Binney

LESSONS IN LIFE

Good luck in life and love, as well as wealth, health and happiness, are the things that we all desire, exactly as our forebears did. Hundreds of sayings relate to these universal concerns, many of them also advising on ways of keeping the wheels of friendship in particular, and society in general, well oiled. Many of these maxims involve superstitions – charms and omens that touch every part of our lives, from day-to-day detail to the big events such as falling in love and marrying. Many also link to the annual round, punctuated by festivals and celebrations. Though these may have their roots in pagan customs, they also have strong connections with religion, as well as with maintaining good relationships with friends and neighbours.

Good advice on how to live your life, and the things you should value, comes from well-known sources such as the Bible's Book of Proverbs and the works of Shakespeare, but also from anonymous sages and, in more recent times, popular songs. While life today may be much more ordered and predictable than it was when many of these sayings originated, chance and superstition still play their parts – which is why so many of us still fear bad luck if we walk under a ladder or break a mirror.

Don't break a mirror:
you'll have seven years of bad luck

This is just one of many superstitions about mirrors, which have been prized for more than 7,000 years. While a broken mirror is also said to foretell a death in the family or the loss of a best friend, the proverbial warning to the vain is that too much gazing in the mirror will make the Devil appear.

It was by polishing the volcanic mineral obsidian that the people of the Middle East and northern Italy made the first mirrors. These were small hand mirrors used during one's personal toilet. Only when the Venetians discovered how to silver glass in the mid-16th century could large mirrors become expensive decorations for the home; the first patent for their manufacture in Britain was obtained in 1615 by Sir Robert Mansell.

Incidentally...

Some of the most valuable antique mirrors are prized for their exceptional frames, made by craftsmen such as Grinling Gibbons, the Dutch-born woodcarver and sculptor of the late 17th and early 18th centuries. In the Georgian period, wall mirrors were also designed by eminent furniture makers such as Chippendale, Sheraton and Hepplewhite.

THE CONVEX MIRROR, OFTEN WITH AN ELABORATELY CARVED FRAME THAT SOMETIMES SUPPORTED CANDLESTICKS, BECAME FASHIONABLE IN THE 1790S, ALTHOUGH IT HAD BEEN MANUFACTURED SINCE THE 16TH CENTURY. IT PRODUCES A PARTICULARLY DISTORTED IMAGE.

STRIKE WHILE THE IRON IS HOT

An encouragement to make the most of your opportunities while they last, this saying has its roots in the blacksmith's shop and resonances in the domestic duties carried out in times past.

Since the Iron Age, which began around 1500 BC, heating iron and beating it while red hot into anything from knife blades to ploughshares has been central to societies around the world. The smith – and the power of his fire – were much revered in many cultures. According to the ancient Romans, the god Vulcan had his workshop in the fiery heart of Mount Etna, Sicily. Eruptions from the volcano were, they believed, the sparks flying from his smithy, where he made thunderbolts for Jupiter, the ruler of the skies.

The first heated domestic irons, which were filled with hot coals, were used in the Far East in the 8th century BC. Box irons of a similar design were used until the 17th century, when solid flatirons, which could be heated directly on the stove, were introduced. Keeping irons hot demanded constant vigilance. If the heat of the stove was allowed to slacken then the irons would be too cool, but the wise laundry maid would make sure she had 'several irons in the fire' to cover every eventuality.

Incidentally…

In the late 19th century there were domestic irons fuelled by kerosene, alcohol, gas and even whale oil, but the first electric irons were patented in the USA by Henry Seely in 1882. The ironing board is said to have been 'invented' by the Vikings, who spread their clothes on whalebone plaques and smoothed them with wooden rollers, but even well into the 20th century many housewives continued to do their ironing on a kitchen table padded with folded sheets or towels.

PIG IRON (IRON MADE IN BLAST FURNACES FROM THE 17TH CENTURY ON) GOT ITS NAME BECAUSE, WHEN THE MOLTEN IRON FLOWING ALONG ONE LARGE CHANNEL RAN INTO MANY SMALLER MOULDS LEADING OFF AT ONE SIDE, IT LOOKED LIKE PIGLETS FEEDING AT THE SOW.

YOU CAN'T MAKE AN OMELETTE WITHOUT BREAKING EGGS

A warning that you cannot get something for nothing and that sacrifices, though they may mean effort, can have tangible rewards. The French name betrays the best-known origin of the dish.

The English spelling 'omelet', first recorded in 1611 to describe 'a pancake of egges', is still used in American cookbooks.

On ne saurait faire une omelette sans casser les oeufs is the original French for this expression. The omelette, however, was probably known to cooks of many countries well before the French coined the word in the 16th century, and has long been enjoyed as a sweet as well as a savoury dish. Experts on Middle Eastern food think that it may originally have come from Persia as a more solid dish called an *eggah* – more like a Spanish tortilla, which typically contains potatoes and onions.

Incidentally...

Omelette Arnold Bennett, made with smoked haddock, is named for the English novelist and drama critic who habitually ate the dish as a post-theatre supper at the Savoy Hotel Grill in London in the 1920s.

On the making of the perfect French omelette, cooks are agreed that the eggs should be very fresh, that they should be cooked in butter, that it is best to keep a special pan for omelette preparation, and that once cooked the omelette should be served immediately. Purists disapprove of the addition of milk advised by the American 19th-century cook Fannie Merritt Farmer. Her 'Plain Omelet', known in England as a soufflé omelette, was made by separating the eggs, beating the whites and folding them into the yolks before cooking to give a puffed-up result. The dish was finished in the oven to allow the top to cook through.

ANOTHER CULINARY WAY OF EXPRESSING THE SAME THOUGHT IS THE PROVERB: 'HE WHO DOES NOT KILL HOGS, WILL NOT GET BLACK PUDDINGS.'

YOU'LL HAVE GOOD LUCK IF A BLACK CAT CROSSES YOUR PATH

It all depends where you live. Black cats are considered lucky in Britain, when you meet them and also when they enter the house uninvited, but in the USA and Europe they are ill omens. There, it is white felines that are the lucky ones.

The Egyptians revered all cats, whatever their colour, for their ability to keep valuable granaries free of rodents. When a cat died it was taken to Bubastis, home of the cat goddess Basht or Pasht, who was also the deity of pleasure and protector against contagious disease, and was believed to have nine lives.

Presumably from the sounds of their voices, pet cats were affectionately known as 'Mau'.

In Europe, cats became the subjects of religious persecution when, in the Middle Ages, they became associated with a form of devil worship in which Satan took the form of a black cat. On the plus side, black cats were believed, in Britain, to have considerable powers of healing. Just the touch of a single hair from a black cat's tail would, it was said, cure a stye, while smearing the blood of a black cat on the rash was recommended to clear up an attack of shingles.

Incidentally...

According to Buddhist lore a rat once ate part of one of the scriptures of the Enlightened One. So the Buddha took a piece of its skin and turned it into a cat. The proof? That rats are still afraid of cats.

Other colourful cat connotations

That a cat may look at a king is an expression of equality.

A catnap is a short doze.

A cat's eye is a reflective stud on the road that shines like the feline eye when illuminated by headlights.

Models tread the narrow catwalk as nimbly as felines.

'The cat's whiskers' is a saying used to descirbe something particularly good – and in reality they are biologically supremely sensitive.

A cats' chorus is a cacophony of sound, like a group of cats mewing and yowling at night.

KISS AND MAKE UP

The kiss is not just a powerful symbol of reconciliation, probably used in the earliest societies, but also an affectionate greeting and an act of intimacy that is an essential part of being human.

It can be no accident that the kiss is such a potent form of touch. Our lips have evolved, with our hands, as the parts of the body most sensitive to physical contact. And because we smell another person as we kiss them, it is also an act of recognition. As the Bible records, the blind Isaac, as an old man, kissed in blessing the person he thought was his son Esau. But Isaac was mistaken. Instead of Esau he kissed Jacob dressed in his brother's clothes – garments that retained Esau's personal odour.

Incidentally...

In a whole range of cultures, including Inuit, Maori and Polynesian, nose rubbing or nose kissing is the equivalent of the western kiss. Describing such behaviour among the Malays in the 1830s, Charles Darwin observed: 'This lasted rather longer than a cordial shake of the hand with us, and as we vary the force of the grasp of the hand in shaking, so do they in pressing,' and that 'during the process they uttered comfortable little grunts.'

The kiss of reconciliation may go back even farther in our evolution, for, after a quarrel, chimpanzees will kiss and embrace to make the peace. Moreover, some anthropologists, including Desmond Morris, author of *Manwatching* (1977), believe that the French kiss evolved from mothers weaning their children by feeding them mouth-to-mouth with pre-chewed morsels, in an exchange similar to that used by birds and other creatures.

Glandular fever, or infectious mononucleosis, a viral disease most common among those between 15 and 17 years old, is known colloquially as the kissing disease from its most likely method of transmission.

YOU CAN TELL A PERSON'S CHARACTER BY THEIR HANDWRITING

And, say the experts, even more than this, when they analyse both the overall impression of a person's writing style and elements such as the size and shape of the letters and the way in which they are joined and embellished.

Beware, says the American specialist Dr Baruch M. Lazewnik, of a graceful, flowing writing style. Its beautiful appearance can mask a manipulative personality. Equally, he warns against characterizing backward or left-sloping writing as betraying a weak character. Rather, he maintains, this handwriting type may indicate a tendency to pull back from emotional attachments. A marked slant to the right, however, is agreed by many graphologists to indicate an extrovert.

Other keys to character in handwriting are angles – the connecting strokes used most often by analytical thinkers – and the loops and flourishes favoured by more artistic personalities. The way in which letters are joined – or not – is a guide to the way a person uses logic and connects thoughts and ideas. A tense person may write with great pressure, giving the pen strokes little variation in light and shade.

It was not just the quality of handwriting that was stressed in the 1933 *News Chronicle* guide to letter writing for housewives. It also maintained that 'You can read character in the trouble that has been taken to form a pleasant phrase, kindness in some happy little thought, and pride and self-respect in clear, legible writing and the way the epistle is set out.'

Incidentally...

Modern graphology was founded by the German psychologist Ludwig Klages. He was a leading member of the Vitalist movement in Germany, started in 1895, which maintained that the laws of physics and chemistry cannot alone explain all we need to know about life.

POLICE FORCES AROUND THE WORLD USE GRAPHOLOGY EXPERTS TO DETECT FORGERIES, ESPECIALLY SIGNATURES, WHICH ARE PARTICULARLY DIFFICULT TO IDENTIFY IF THE FORGER HAS SUCCESSFULLY MANAGED TO MIMIC A VICTIM'S WRITING HABITS.

WALKING UNDER LADDERS BRINGS BAD LUCK

Apart from the obvious risk of having something dropped on you by the person on the ladder, the association between ladders and misfortune also goes back to the old practice of hanging criminals – particularly at Tyburn in London – by making them climb a ladder to the gallows.

After death, the ghosts of the condemned were believed to loiter under the place where they had died, so the spot was one to avoid.

Conversely, some people believe that a ladder placed against a wall creates a space that should not be trespassed in because it forms a triangle with the wall and the ground – a sign for the Trinity (Father, Son and Holy Ghost) – and so is sacred.

Accidents with ladders are commonplace. In Britain about 50 people a year are killed by them and over 30,000 need hospital treatment. Causes include

Ladder superstitions

If you walk under a ladder you should spit over your left shoulder to avoid subsequent misfortune.

Walking under a ladder will prevent you from getting married that year.

If you have no choice but to walk under a ladder, make a wish first, and your wish will come true.

Cross your fingers to negate bad luck if you have to walk under a ladder. Or cross your fingers and keep them crossed until you see a dog.

erecting ladders near power lines or in doorways, or on uneven ground, and standing on the topmost rungs. A household guide published in the 1930s advised that when manoeuvring a long ladder the 'amateur should, in all cases of doubt, attach a strong rope to the top of the ladder so it can be controlled.'

In the days before cheap, disposable tights, and especially in wartime, a ladder in an expensive pair of nylon stockings was a disaster. Women soon discovered that a dab of clear nail polish would stop a small ladder and prevent it from running any farther.

It is better to be punctual than to be sorry

Good timekeeping may seem an oppressive discipline, but undoubtedly keeps the wheels of society and business well oiled. Punctuality is, as the French say, 'the politeness of princes' but any hostess is justified in being alarmed by guests who arrive before the appointed hour.

For an informal dinner, says American manners guru Emily Post, 'You should arrive within 15 minutes of the time for which you were invited. More delay than that indicates that you have not made much effort, and it may ruin a hostess's carefully planned meal.' For dating, America's 'Miss Manners' advises men on a first date to 'pick the lady up when you said you would'.

For the theatre, opera house and concert hall – and even the cinema – punctuality is not only polite but necessary to avoid tripping over other members of the audience in the dark. But it is absolutely essential to be on time if you are invited to a reception or to be presented to royalty, members of the government or at the White House. Then the rule is always to be a few minutes early.

Religion was a driving force in timekeeping of old, as in ancient Egyptian and Greek temples, and by the Middle Ages church clocks would call monks to prayer. The need for minute-perfect punctuality on a national scale came with the introduction of railway timetables, which quickly became synonymous with George Bradshaw, the Manchester printer who published the first complete national timetable for all Britain's rail services in 1839. Before that, clocks were set by the sun and could therefore show different times in different parts of the country.

Incidentally...

Throughout the 19th century, in both Britain and the USA, women would stay at home on certain afternoons each week. This time was set aside to receive callers, who would have previously delivered their calling cards, and who could arrive at any time up to four o'clock, or five at the latest.

THROW SPILT SALT OVER YOUR SHOULDER

I t is testament to salt's great value that its spilling should herald ill luck. But, fortunately for the clumsy, it has been a long-held belief that throwing salt over your shoulder can act as an effective antidote.

Ancient suspicions surrounding spilt salt agree that it can bring on all kinds of disaster – from a fallen roof to a fatal wound. Its association with misfortune is thought by some to originate from the depiction by Leonardo da Vinci, in *The Last Supper*, of the traitor Judas turning over the salt cellar, though it is more likely to have arisen in an attempt to deter the careless from wasting such a valuable commodity.

The original salt cellar was a large bowl or 'saler' placed in the centre of the table. In the 16th and 17th centuries the bowl was replaced by large and impressive 'steeple' cellars made of silver, crystal or some other valuable material and often

Incidentally...

To sit above the salt – that is between the salt and the head of the household – was a mark of a guest's distinction. Servants always sat below the salt, along with guests of little regard.

decorated with gold or even precious stones. The use of numerous small salt cellars on a large dining table came into vogue after about 1700, and even in the early 20th century etiquette still called for one salt cellar (with a pepper pot) to be set at every other place for a formal dinner, so that no one need suffer the indignity of having to ask their neighbour to pass the salt.

SALT, THOUGH EXPENSIVE, WAS ESSENTIAL FOR USE AS A PRESERVATIVE IN THE ANCIENT WORLD. THE WORD 'SALARY' COMES FROM THE SALT RATION, OR SALARIUM, GIVEN BY THE ROMANS TO SOLDIERS AND CIVIL SERVANTS, MAKING SALT A FORM OF CURRENCY.

More remedies for avoiding bad luck from spilling salt

Put a little more salt on a knife and let it fall to the ground.

Throw it over your head.

Fling some into the fire, throwing it over your left shoulder.

Throw some of the salt over your shoulder and make the sign of the cross in what remains on the table.

NEVER LOOK A GIFT HORSE IN THE MOUTH

This proverbial advice on gratitude has its origins in the time-honoured practice of judging a horse's age by its teeth. As a horse ages, its gums recede at a steady rate, making the creature literally 'long in the tooth'.

An adult horse with its full dentition has between 36 and 40 teeth. On either side of each jaw are three incisors or 'cutting teeth' and six molars or 'grinders', in front of which is a gap where the bit is placed inside the horse's mouth.

Incidentally...

In mythology the horse is a symbol of courage, which makes it no accident that St George is always depicted on horseback.

Males also have four small canines or 'dog teeth'. Within two weeks of its birth a foal develops 'nippers', or central teeth, and a full set of milk teeth (shed during the third year) is in place by six months. The males acquire their canines in the fourth year and the set of permanent teeth is complete by the age of six.

At seven years old a hook begins to show on the corner incisors on the upper jaw and at eight years a 'dental star' appears on the central incisors.

All these developments allow the horse's age to be determined with relative accuracy. Thereafter it becomes more difficult to age a horse, but experts look for 'Galvayne's grooves', dark markings on the incisors that appear at the age of ten and reach all the way down the corner teeth by the time the animal is 20.

Unlike human teeth, a horse's molars have evolved to carry on growing as fast as they wear down at the crowns. This is an adaptation to a diet of grass, because the sharp silica it contains rapidly destroys teeth enamel.

TO TAKE THE BIT BETWEEN YOUR TEETH IS TO TAKE CONTROL OF A SITUATION. THE EXPRESSION COMES FROM THE TENDENCY OF SOME HORSES TO SET THEIR JAW AGAINST THE BIT AND IGNORE THE COMMANDS OF THE RIDER, THOUGH A HORSE WILL RARELY GRAB THE BIT WITH ITS MOLARS.

DON'T WEAR GREEN AT WEDDINGS

G reen is an unlucky marriage colour: after green, it is said, comes black. The belief may come from the association of green with the mischief wrought by green-clad elves and fairies.

According to William Henderson's *Notes on the Folk Lore of the Northern Counties of England and the Borders* of 1866, nothing green should appear at a wedding, and even 'kale and all other green vegetables' should be excluded from the wedding dinner. Blue, by contrast, is a lucky colour, for as the traditional verse goes: 'Those dressed in blue have lovers true; in green and white, forsaken quite.' Blue is the colour of the sky and of healing, and is also worn by a baby boy (see page 190).

Incidentally...

The new husband carries his wife across the threshold to avoid the bad luck of stumbling at the entrance to her new home.

Warding off evil spirits at weddings in particular, and in life in general, has a long tradition. Fairies are believed to enter a house down the chimney or through a keyhole at night and harm the people sleeping in a house. Elves were believed to kill animals by throwing 'elf-shot' – stones that embedded themselves into the creatures and killed them. At Roman weddings, the witnesses dressed like the bride and groom to confuse any evil spirits besetting the ceremony.

Other ill omens to avoid on wedding days

The bride and groom seeing each other before they meet at church.

The bride bursting a seam on her dress (this means she will be ill-treated by her husband).

The wedding party meeting a funeral cortège on the way to or from the church.

Marrying in Lent.

A dog passing between the couple.

An open grave in the churchyard.

The bride wearing new shoes.

MODERATION IN ALL THINGS

A maxim for the health of body, mind and spirit, stemming from the teaching of the ancient Greek philosopher Epicurus of Samos, this sentiment is now endorsed by many of today's health professionals and diet gurus.

Pleasure, maintained Epicurus, who lived from 341 to 270 BC, was the highest good, and 'indulgence which presents a greater pleasure or produces a greater pain is to be avoided'. Which means that moderation satisfies the Epicurean ideal of a lifetime of happiness. Beyond a certain maximum, he stipulated, it is impossible for pleasure to increase in intensity; he named this peak of experience ataraxia, meaning 'without disturbance'. When the English language took over the word 'epicurean', however, the single idea of pleasure as the highest good was emphasized without the qualification of moderation, so that today the words 'epicure' and 'epicurean' have the connotations of 'eat, drink and be merry' that Epicurus and his followers so deplored.

The Victorian handbook *Enquire Within Upon Everything* summed up the saying like this: 'Moderation in eating and drinking, short hours of labour and study, regularity in exercise, recreation and rest, cleanliness, equanimity of temper and equality of temperature – these are the great essentials to that which surpasses all wealth, health of mind and body.'

In the modern age of extreme diets, evidence continues to mount in favour of the moderate 'meat and two veg' philosophy of eating, along with regular exercise that is sufficient to get the heart working and feel-good endorphins flowing – but not enough to strain the hamstrings or wear away the cartilages. Also advised is a healthy balance between work and play.

Incidentally...

In many religions, periods of fasting, such as Lent and Ramadan, are preceded and/or ended with indulgent festivals. In the Christian tradition, Lent begins with Shrove or 'Fat' Tuesday (Mardi Gras) and ends with Easter's roast lamb, chocolate eggs and marzipan-filled and topped simnel cake.

MANNERS MAKETH MAN – AND WOMAN TOO

Though the addendum to the saying is modern, the first part of it comes from a 15th-century book of manners, *The Babees' Book*. Rules for good behaviour, however, can be traced back to the earliest civilizations.

'Be prudent when you open your mouth,' said the Egyptian Ptahhotep in his *Instructions* written in around 2350 BC, a treatise that laid down the first known rules of manners. 'Be not arrogant because of that which you know; deal with the ignorant as with the learned.'

Much later, a complex system of etiquette evolved with the rules of precedence established in Anglo-Saxon courts of the 10th century and, especially, in the three centuries that followed, with the ideal of chivalry – encompassing service, the protection of vulnerable individuals, and fidelity — that was enacted by the knights who fought in the Crusades.

Historically, a gentleman was a man of good (that is, high) birth, and his wife was automatically a lady. But because the rank of gentleman could be acquired through both wealth and landowning, as well as by noble deeds, the distinction between status and manners became, and has remained, blurred. By the 19th century the rules of good manners were strongly tilted towards the likes and dislikes of the middle class rather than the aristocracy.

Incidentally...

In 1526 the Dutch scholar Desiderius Erasmus, writing for the instruction of the sons of the aristocracy in his De Civilitate Morum Puerilium *('On Civility in Boys') covered everything from dental hygiene and the importance of clean fingernails at the dinner table to when and how to spit.*

Victorian manners

The 19th-century list of dos and don'ts of good manners for both men and women was endless. This is a small selection:

Be decorous and neat.

Be affable and studious to please.

Hide your rank from someone inferior.

Do not be haughty, unkind or overbearing.

Avoid drunkenness.

Beware of foppery and flirtation.

Dress well, do not be slovenly.

Prefer to listen than to talk.

Avoid manifestations of ill temper.

And, for women, avoid displaying an excess of jewellery.

FAIR EXCHANGE IS NO ROBBERY

The roots of this expression of fair play lie in barter or 'silent trade' – the exchange of goods that predates the invention of money. Far from being an outmoded system, barter is now coming back into fashion, with millions of participants worldwide.

Incidentally...

Though pictorial cigarette cards first appeared in the 1880s, their exchange reached its heyday in the 1930s. For today's collectors the most prized sets are those such as Wills' Waterloo, created to mark the battle's centenary in June 1915. Because at the time the French were Britain's allies in World War I, these were never issued, but a few rare sets survive.

In the very earliest societies, barter involved the necessities of life, with furs, skins and fish hooks being swapped for food and fire. Other items valued for barter included practical things such as spears and knives, and rice, yams and other crops, but also decorative beads, ivory and jade.

The world's first 'currencies' were cattle and grain which, from around 9000 BC, acquired specific values. The Babylonians deposited grain in state granaries and issued receipts of deposit in the form of clay tablets which could be used to 'pay' for other things.

In ancient China, cowrie shells were used as currency from 1500 BC, and the same shells were employed as such on many Pacific Islands until relatively recently. But silver was the first real money, used in Mesopotamia some 4,000 years ago. Goods such as wool, grain and oil were weighed and traded for a set amount of this precious metal.

BOTH MONEY AND THE MINT IN WHICH IT IS STRUCK GET THEIR NAMES FROM JUNO MONETA, THE ROMAN GODDESS OF ABUNDANCE AND ADVISOR TO THOSE ABOUT TO MARRY.

BEAUTY IS IN THE EYE OF THE BEHOLDER

Meaning that, whether skin deep or not, beauty is purely subjective, especially to the lovelorn and to proud parents. But mathematics may have the last word, for many of the world's most beautiful objects obey the rules of the golden ratio.

If you don't think you're beautiful don't worry, for all cats, they say, are grey in the dark!

The golden ratio works like this. Take any two numbers and add them together (say 10 + 9). Then add the result (19) to the second number (9 + 19 = 28). Then do the same again (19 + 28 = 47). Whatever the sequence, the ratio of the last two numbers is close to the golden ratio of **1.618033989…**; beyond the decimal point there is always an infinite string of numbers.

Without being aware of it, we judge the appearance of objects by the closeness with which their proportions approximate to the golden ratio. It occurs widely in nature, and artists and architects from the Renaissance on have used it to achieve aesthetically satisfying works.

Incidentally…

In the original version of the story Beauty and the Beast *by Madame Gabrielle de Villeneuve, first published in France in 1740, the beast turns back into the Prince only after, and not before, the wedding night.*

WHAT WORTH BEAUTY? ACCORDING TO AN OLD CHINESE PROVERB, IF YOU HAVE ONLY TWO PENNIES LEFT IN THE WORLD YOU SHOULD BUY A LOAF OF BREAD WITH ONE AND A LILY WITH THE OTHER.

SLEEP ON IT

This advice is now proven to be the quickest way of problem-solving but it has long been held anecdotally to be the surest way to soothe worries as well as refreshing both body and mind.

Between 1909 and 1916 the Reverend Nehemiah Curnock, an English parson, published eight volumes in which he deciphered the 18th-century *Journal* of John Wesley, the founder of Methodism, which was originally written in code. Having bought a Bible annotated in the same code, he studied it for days, but had no success in finding the solution.

Then one night he dreamed that he was reading the 'clear' deciphered text and, when he awoke, found that he had cracked the code.

Incidentally…

The habit of young and old sleeping together, so that the vitality of the former may rub off on the latter, goes back to Biblical times. The attendants of the old King David brought him a young virgin, Abishag, to lie in his arms and make him warm; she did not lose her virginity.

January 2004 saw the publication of studies by a group of German scientists, working in Cologne and Lübeck, who devised an elegant experiment to prove the saying. First they set trained volunteers a maths problem that could be solved in seven steps or, using a neat shortcut, in only three. Having been presented with the task, some volunteers were allowed to sleep, others were not. Eight hours later, 13 of the 22 people who had slept worked out the shortcut compared with five of the 22 who had not.

The key, say the experts, is that sleep reorganizes information in the brain, affecting the way it is remembered and processed. But whether dreams are also necessary to our wellbeing has yet to be proved. Certainly many creative people do their best work early in the morning. Samuel Taylor Coleridge claimed to have written the poem 'Kubla Khan' (subtitled 'A Vision in a Dream') in its entirety directly after waking from opium-induced slumber.

FORGIVE AND FORGET

One of the most difficult of life's lessons, but as Mahatma Gandhi (1869–1948) said: 'The weak can never forgive. Forgiveness is the attribute of the strong.'

Aside from religious teachings such as Christianity, in which the principle of forgiveness is central, the poet Decimus Magnus Ausonius, a native of Bordeaux who became a Roman consul in AD 379, put the solution firmly in the court of the individual: 'Forgive many things in others,' he advised, 'nothing in yourself.'

The value of forgiveness, say the psychologists, is that it allows the shattered soul to move on, to recover and, even if it takes many years, to attain a new and comfortable rhythm of life. Forgiveness is also thought to help offenders. But should we also forget? For emotional restoration, probably not, say many experts. Revenge – the Old Testament 'eye for an eye' – may be temporarily satisfying, whether it is served hot or cold, but is usually ineffective in salving sores in the long term.

Incidentally...

On the lighter side, according to the 19th-century poet and playwright Oscar Wilde, you should 'Never forgive your enemies; nothing annoys them so much.' The wry observation of the novelist W. Somerset Maugham in The Moon and Sixpence, *published in 1919, was that 'A woman can forgive a man for the harm he does her... but she can never forgive him for the sacrifices he makes on her account.'*

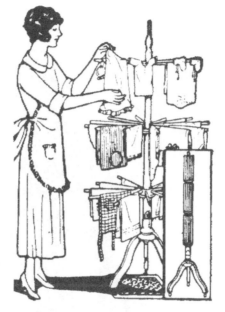

BETTER
HOUSEKEEPING

As soon as people started to make homes – the earliest we know of are some 10,000 years old, in the Middle East and at Çatal Hüyük, now in Turkey – the need for housekeeping began. Though the links between dirt and disease would not be identified until centuries later, we know that early people swept their floors, washed clothes and had storerooms for food and specific areas for sleeping and cooking.

As homes evolved, living space changed from a single room or 'hall' to a series of smaller rooms. By the 19th century keeping house had become a full-time occupation. For the better off it necessitated a plethora of servants, from housekeepers to laundry maids. *Mrs Beeton's Book of Household Management* of 1861 provided sound advice, as did the growing number of other practical publications.

Thanks to devices such as the washing machine and vacuum cleaner, the housework no longer takes all week, but we still share many of the problems of our grandmothers. Moths still chew our clothes, mice still invade our living space, windows still need cleaning. Despite the plethora of new products, many of the old remedies are still the best.

Set a cat to catch a mouse

The ancient Egyptians kept cats in their granaries to kill mice and rats. Some 3,500 years on, felines are still effective against these household pests, though a really bad rodent infestation may require the intervention of a professional controller.

Cat versus mouse is a matter of instinct. A cat is 'programmed' to chase and torment a mouse (or a fluff-filled replica or even a rolled-up pair of socks until it tires of the deception), and while a pet cat may present you with dead rodents as 'gifts', its untamed ancestors would have relied on these creatures for food. And although a cat will hunt during the day, at heart it is a night hunter, using its natural attributes of reflective eyes, acute hearing, sharp claws and long canine teeth to detect and seize its prey. Cats also have the patience to wait for hours for their prey and to torment it until it is finally dead.

IN THE MUCH LOVED CARTOON *TOM AND JERRY* IT IS THE MOUSE THAT OFTEN WINS THE DUEL OF WITS.

Mice rely for their evolutionary success on safety in numbers (ensured by rapid and persistent breeding), agility and an omnivorous diet that can even include newspapers and electric cables. They are also intelligent enough to work out how to get out of the most cunning mousetraps and shun all but the most tempting of chemical baits.

Incidentally...

Because of their association with witches and the Devil, cats were routinely exterminated from the 13th century onwards. It is possible that the Great Plague, which struck London in 1664, would not have happened if there had been enough cats available to catch the rats that transmitted the disease.

Mouse-catching tips

If you can't or won't keep a cat, try one of these methods of catching or deterring mice:

Block up their exits and entrances – including the smallest gaps under doors, between floorboards and around pipes.

Smear mint toothpaste round the edges of their holes: the smell will deter them.

Bait mousetraps with bacon or nut chocolate rather than cheese.

Put down proprietary mousekiller, but be sure to keep poisons away from food and children. Handle any deceased animals wearing rubber gloves.

DE-SCALE A KETTLE WITH VINEGAR

The classroom chemistry of acid plus alkali is the secret behind this effective tip, which is sure to save you money on expensive proprietary preparations. Lemon juice also works well in both kettles and showerheads.

Limescale, made primarily of alkaline calcium carbonate, is deposited as 'fur' in your kettle (and dishwasher, washing machine and toilet) if you live in a hard water area. Dissolved calcium compounds separate out as the water is boiled, and eventually accumulate as solid lumps.

Vinegar, which is acetic acid (or lemon juice, which is citric acid) reacts with limescale and dissolves it. For bad scaling, fill the kettle with a mixture of malt or white pickling vinegar diluted half and half with water, bring it to the boil and leave it for a couple of hours or overnight. If any furring remains, simply repeat the process.

Incidentally...

An old remedy for preventing kettles from furring up was to place a marble, pebble or oyster shell inside the kettle to 'catch' the scale. A ball of wire mesh does the same job.

Never eat a boiled egg with a silver spoon

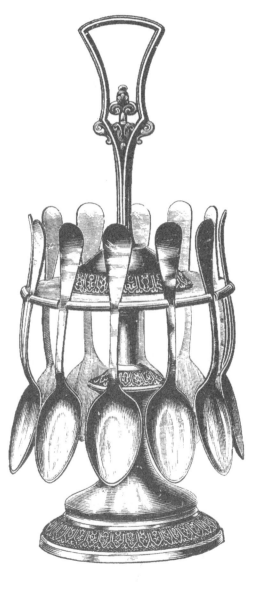

The quickest way to tarnish silver is to use it to eat an egg. Not only that, but the reaction between the silver and the egg will create a foul taste in the mouth. Vegetables that are high in sulphur, such as cabbage, will also quickly tarnish silver.

When silver comes in contact with hydrogen sulphide — the 'bad eggs' gas that dissipates from a yolk — it forms blue-black silver sulphide, or tarnish. Washing up directly after a meal will help prevent tarnishing, and for taking a little tarnish off sterling silver the quickest and easiest remedy is to soak it in hot water to which you have added a teaspoon of washing or baking soda.

A JEWELLER'S ROUGE CLOTH IS THE NEAREST MODERN EQUIVALENT TO THE OLD METHOD OF CLEANING SILVER. IN FORMER TIMES THE ROUGE WOULD HAVE BEEN BOUGHT AS A POWDER AND MIXED WITH AMMONIA BEFORE USE.

For a high shine, you can buff silver with a cloth or a chamois leather, but this risks wearing away the coating of EPS or 'silver plate'. To treat a heavy tarnish the experts advise against immersing silver in an acid 'dip'. If used at all, it is best applied sparingly on a sponge soaked in the solution and washed off in very hot water immediately afterwards.

NEVER KEEP SALT IN AN UNLINED SILVER CELLAR FOR LONGER THAN A FEW HOURS. THE SALT WILL EAT AWAY AT — OR 'PIT' — THE METAL.

Sterling silver is 92.5 per cent pure silver with 7.5 per cent copper added to make a more durable alloy. Silver plate is a thin film of silver electroplated on to a base metal object after manufacture.

DON'T DRY WET SHOES BY THE FIRE

Soaked leather, if dried quickly, will become brittle and cracked and develop white 'tide marks'. The old way is still the best way: sponge wet shoes, stuff them with crumpled newspaper and leave them to dry slowly and naturally.

There is nothing more frustrating than having a good pair of shoes ruined by rain or snow, and an old way of waterproofing them was to rub them with castor oil or petroleum jelly or with a mixture of beeswax and lard. Paraffin oil was added to boot blacking to protect and restore damp leather, while varnishing the soles of boots was said to 'render them impervious to damp and make them last longer'.

In the days before mass manufacture, leather boots and shoes were valuable items. Durable clogs, with iron-shod wooden soles and leather or fabric uppers, were a cheaper and more hard-wearing alternative for most working people in Britain. In the Netherlands and other continental European countries, all-wood clogs were worn. In wartime Britain – and in post-war years when clothes were still rationed – it was commonplace for children to have a single pair of shoes for the winter from which the toes were later cut out to make 'sandals' for the summer.

To keep good footwear in shape, boot or shoe trees are still the best treatment, and a bespoke men's shoemaker will still supply trees to fit shoes exactly. Suede that has become shiny can easily be restored by carefully rubbing it with fine sandpaper.

POLISH WINDOWS WITH NEWSPAPER

Rolled into a pad, newspaper is a good old-fashioned substitute for a polishing cloth or chamois leather, but it is by no means the only effective way to get the shine on your panes that was once essential to a good reputation. 'Dirty windows', it was said, 'speak to the passer-by of the negligence of the inmates.'

Dirty windows not only deprive rooms of light but make them look unattractive. If you can, clean the windows when the sun is not shining on the glass, to prevent streaks and allow you to see the results of your labours clearly.

Good modern cleaning choices are either washing with a solution of detergent or a proprietary liquid, or using a spray containing ammonia and alcohol, which then needs to be rubbed off with a soft cloth. The squeegee, used by the professionals, is an excellent — and some say the only — means of getting a sparkling finish on your windows.

Don't forget the frames. Regular dusting helps to keep them free of dirt, but in winter it is also essential to remove any condensation that accumulates on them: as well as rotting wooden frames, it can be the breeding ground for unsightly black mildew.

Incidentally...

Despite its name, chamois leather is not made from goatskin but from the underlayer or 'split' of a sheepskin after the top layer has been removed.

Old window-cleaning recipes

Equal parts of paraffin and methylated spirits, rubbed on to the dry glass and polished off with a soft cloth when dry.

A bunch of stinging nettles dipped into water with a dash of vinegar added (wear thick gloves!). Dry the glass with a soft cloth or chamois.

Turpentine: this is especially good for grease marks.

A solution made by pouring boiling water on a chopped potato.

Washing soda dissolved in water, with a little ammonia added.

NEVER SOAK KNIFE HANDLES IN HOT WATER

A mantra for perfect washing up. The simple reason is that hot water loosens the glue used to stick the handle to the knife. It also discolours, cracks and splits ivory and bone, the traditional materials for handles.

Special treatment for knives once extended much further. Victorian scullery maids would have been under strict instructions to wash blades and handles separately, or to soak blades in a jar of water rather than immersing them, and to use a little salt to remove stains from knife handles. Before the advent of stainless steel, knives were rubbed with mutton fat after they had been washed and dried to prevent them from rusting. Blades were kept bright by rubbing them on a knife board covered in brick dust, which was then carefully removed from the handles using a cloth.

Stainless steel was created in 1913 by the Sheffield metallurgist and cutlery maker Harry Brearley, and it was he who made the Yorkshire city synonymous with steel.

Knives, with spoons, are the most ancient pieces of cutlery. Forks were added as tableware from Georgian times, although the Romans used two-pronged forks for serving. Knives were so valuable that until the 16th century a family would share one knife between them, passing it around the table, then eat their food with a spoon or their fingers, or sup directly from a bowl. Guests would bring their own knives to the table.

NEVER LET KNIVES CROSS WHEN PLACED ON THE TABLE OR YOU WILL INVOKE BAD LUCK, OR EVEN DISASTER.

Incidentally…

The first knives were made from bones, flints and obsidian, a kind of volcanic 'glass'. Obsidian blades are many times sharper than steel ones, and are now used in surgery.

GET GREASE MARKS OFF CLOTHES BY IRONING THEM OVER BLOTTING PAPER

The theory is that the heat of the iron will melt the grease – on carpets as well as clothes – which will then be absorbed by the blotting paper. In practice, however, if you try this you need to be careful you don't 'cook' the mark and make it even more difficult to remove.

For washable clothes, the best way to get rid of grease marks (made by anything from mayonnaise to machine oil) is to wash them with detergent in the hottest water possible. Pre-wash treatment with a proprietary stain remover will also help, but make sure you test the fabric first to be certain it is colourfast. Take anything that can't be washed to the dry cleaners and

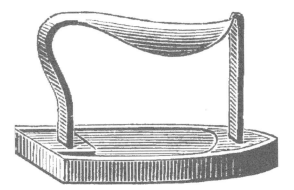

In the days before the existence of household detergents, another recommended method was to rub dry flour on a garment or carpet and to leave it for several hours to absorb any grease or oil. Turpentine was also used as a dry cleaner.

highlight the offending areas for special treatment. For carpets and rugs, carpet shampoos are most effective, either for spot cleaning of grease stains or all-over cleaning.

On grease, detergents are much more effective than soap because they not only act to emulsify the fat – break it up into minute droplets which will lift off the fibres of a fabric – but, as they do so, attach themselves selectively to dirt. The first detergents were developed in Germany in the 1880s, and Nekal was the first brand name detergent, sold there in 1917.

CANDLE WAX MAY BE MORE EASILY REMOVED IF IT IS FIRST HARDENED WITH A BLOCK OF ICE SO THAT MOST OF IT CAN BE CHIPPED OFF. ANY REMAINS CAN THEN BE GIVEN THE 'HOT IRON AND BLOTTING PAPER' TREATMENT. THE CHILLING PROCESS IS ALSO RECOMMENDED FOR THE REMOVAL OF CHEWING GUM.

POLISH FURNITURE WITH BEESWAX

Natural beeswax is still one of the best polishes for keeping wooden furniture in great condition, though special finishes need other kinds of treatment.

Waxing and polishing furniture protects it and keeps it looking shiny and bright. It won't need re-treating more than once or twice a year, depending on how often it is used. Once well waxed, with a bought or home-made polish (see below) it can be cleaned with a duster (aided if you wish by a proprietary dusting spray) or wiped with a barely damp cloth. Furniture finished with shellac, lacquer or varnish is better left unwaxed. Soapy water used sparingly on a soft cloth should remove all but the worst marks.

You can make a good all-purpose beeswax mixture at home by melting 2 tablespoons of beeswax granules with the same quantity of turpentine. Oak furniture that is stained or dull will take on a wonderful shine if polished with a warm mixture of one tablespoon of beeswax granules melted with $^1/_2$ pint of (300ml) beer and two teaspoons of sugar.

Incidentally...

Camouflage is the best way of dealing with scratches and other marks on furniture. Buy one of the 'touch up' pens sold for the purpose or try a small amount of artist's oil paint on a cotton bud or fine brush, or some cream shoe polish in a matching colour applied in the same way.

CLEANLINESS IS NEXT TO GODLINESS

T his mantra of the diligent housewife was first declared by John Wesley, the 18th-century founder of Methodism. In the same sermon he also declared neatness of apparel to be 'a duty, not a sin'.

At the time of John Wesley's pronouncement, cleaning was a daily routine that relied on elbow grease combined with a range of home-made materials including a paste of ashes, sand and grit for scouring, a polish for grates made from bone ash and charcoal, and a beeswax furniture polish.

Soap was a luxury reserved for personal use, though surfaces might be scrubbed with lye, an alkali made from ashes. Cleaning was made more difficult by the clutter deemed necessary in the well-appointed middle class home and by the smoke from coal fires.

As to godliness, it is thought that Wesley's saying came originally from an ancient rabbi, Phinehas ben Yair, and for the ancient Jews cleanliness meant much more than the absence of dirt. Washing was a religious ritual for, as it says in the Talmud, 'Respect for God demands that the face, the hands and the feet be washed every day.' There were – and still are for devout Jews – many sources of uncleanliness, including foods such as pork, shellfish, and the blood of any animal.

This Victorian rhyme about laundry epitomizes the strong connection made at the time between dirt and guilt:

> *They that wash on Monday*
> *Have all the week to dry.*
> *They that wash on Tuesday*
> *Are not so much awry.*
> *They that wash on Wednesday*
> *Are not so much to blame.*
> *They that wash on Thursday*
> *Wash for very shame.*
> *They that wash on Friday*
> *Wash in sorry need.*
> *They that wash on Saturday*
> *Oh they are sluts indeed.*

And of course no one would ever have contemplated doing their washing on a Sunday when they should have been at church!

USE LAVENDER TO KEEP CLOTHES MOTHS AT BAY

L avender will keep your drawers and wardrobes smelling sweet, but as a moth deterrent it is not nearly as effective as some traditionalists would have you believe. For a natural choice, cedar oil is a better remedy, but is still far from totally reliable.

The clothes moth is a menace. It lays its eggs on the fibres of clothes and carpets, where they hatch into larvae about ¼in (6mm) long, which then plump themselves up by munching holes in your prized garments and furnishings. Wool is their favourite food, but they will also devour cotton and even leather and fur. The moths that hatch from the larvae don't eat at all, but are ready to mate and restart the cycle.

Incidentally...

In northern England clothes moths are sometimes known as 'ghosts'. Killing one is thought to precipitate the death of a relative.

Camphor oil was the original ingredient of mothballs, but it has been superseded by more powerful and effective chemicals, such as naphthalene and parachlorobenzene. If you use them, follow any instructions to the letter.

Cleanliness was, and is, the most effective way of protecting items from moths, which are particularly attracted to food and grease on clothes. Keeping woollens well brushed (skin flakes are additional food) will help them stay moth-free, and ironing may kill the eggs.

The 1920s housewife was advised to get rid of carpet moths by scrubbing the floor with '...hot water made exceedingly salty before replacing the carpet, and sprinkle the carpet once a week before sweeping until the pests disappear.' The beating of rugs, a household duty now replaced by vacuuming, was a standard part of the weekly cleaning routine.

Dry cleaning will help to mothproof clothes. Alternatively, try putting them in the freezer, wrapped in a plastic bag, for ten days.

NEW BROOMS SWEEP CLEAN

Another way of saying that change is a good thing, for the housewife it is also a reminder that her cleaning utensils should be renewed regularly.

Appropriately, the broom shares its name with the flexible branches of the plants long used for cleaning (botanically the genera *Cytisus* and *Genista*) for it was these, as well as branches of birch and heather, and tufts of maize, that

were probably employed to sweep the floors of early dwellings. Tied together, and with a handle added, bundles of these twigs became the besom.

The wooden broom with bundles of bristles glued into its head dates back to the 15th century, and was still vital to the cleaning repertoire long after the invention of the vacuum cleaner by the London engineer Hubert Cecil Booth in the early 20th century. Brush purchasers of the 1930s were advised to look out for the presence of 'inferior mixtures' hidden in a broom. These, it was advised, should be identified 'by placing the hand across the surface of the broom and noting the greater readiness with which the bristle will spring back when released, as compared with the less springy substitute'.

Broom myths

Dozens of old sayings relate to the buying and handling of brooms – apart, of course, from their use as transportation for both witches and their feline familiars:

Brooms bought in May sweep the family away.

If you set a broom in the corner, strangers will come to the house.

Lay a broom across the doorway to protect the house.

Throw a broom to ward off witches.

It is unlucky to put a sweeping brush on a table.

A servant will not get her wages if the head comes off her broom while she is sweeping.

A BOILED CORK
WILL FIT ANY BOTTLE

This old tip works because boiling water softens the cork. Although it also makes it swell, the cork becomes malleable enough to be forced into a narrow opening. Modern wine makers soften sterilized corks in a mixture of glycerol and sulphur dioxide before they are rammed home.

The Romans used corks to seal their wine jars, but putting wine in corked bottles has been usual only since the late 17th century, when it was discovered that wine kept and matured much better this way than if left in the barrel. Wine makers of that time also quickly realized that bottles needed to be laid horizontally to prevent the cork from drying out: a dry cork lets in air, which oxidizes the wine and makes it vinegary.

Incidentally...

Keeping a cork in your pocket during the day, and under your pillow at night, is said to be an effective way of keeping cramp at bay. In the 19th century people even made protective garters of thin discs of cork sewn between silk ribbons.

Natural cork comes from the thick, protective bark of the evergreen cork oak (*Quercus suber*), native to the western Mediterranean. It is cultivated particularly in Portugal, which still supplies a large proportion of the market. What makes the cork such an effective stopper is the combination of a honeycomb of minute air cells (over half the volume of cork is empty space) and the waxy, waterproof substance suberin found in its cell walls. The structure of cork was first seen under the microscope by the English scientist Robert Hooke in the 1660s.

The increasing use of the plastic 'cork' has as much to do with the incidence of corked wines — wines that are tainted with the chemical trichloroanisole, usually as the result of rotten or mouldy corks — as with the increasing scarcity and expense of the natural material.

AN OLD TIP FOR A CORK THAT IS A LITTLE TOO LARGE FOR THE BOTTLE IS TO ROLL IT ON THE FLOOR AND PRESS ON IT WITH THE SOLE OF A BOOT OR HEAVY SHOE.

REVIVE CUT FLOWERS BY DIPPING THE STEMS IN HOT WATER

This shock treatment works for flowers with woody stems and some soft-stemmed blooms including dahlias, hellebores and anemones — and for roses limp at the neck. Afterwards, stems need to be left in cold water for a couple of hours before being arranged in a vase.

Incidentally…

To prevent indelible marks on valuable furniture, carpets and clothes, it is wise to remove the stamens of lilies before the flowers are arranged, though this reduces their heady scent and diminishes their looks.

Flowers go limp because they lack water, often because air bubbles get trapped in their stems. Water at boiling point is recommended for this conditioning treatment: immersion for no more than 30 seconds pushes water quickly up the stems. Ideally, the flower heads and leaves should be loosely wrapped in a clean cloth to prevent them from being damaged by steam. For flowers such as poppies and euphorbias, which exude a milky latex, the recommended heat treatment is not boiling but singeing, to prevent the loss of fluid. Simply hold the cut end of the stalk in a candle or match flame until it is blackened and no more liquid oozes out.

Flower arrangers also use other ruses to help make flowers last longer. These include slitting woody stems and scraping off the bark, and submerging leaves (except grey, furry ones) and stems in water for a couple of hours. Putting an aspirin in the vase with cut flowers can prevent wilting, because it has the effect of closing off the stomata, or pores, on the leaf surfaces through which water vapour naturally escapes.

THE JAPANESE ART OF IKEBANA BEGAN WITH THE CUSTOM OF OFFERING FLOWERS TO BUDDHA IN THE 6TH CENTURY. ALL IKEBANA ARRANGEMENTS ARE ASYMMETRICAL, SYMBOLIZING THE BALANCE OF OPPOSITES, AND CONSIST OF THREE MAIN 'LINES'. *SHIN*, REPRESENTING HEAVEN, IS THE LONGEST LINE, *SOE*, THE MIDDLE LINE, SYMBOLIZES MAN WHILE THE SHORTEST LINE, *HIKAE*, REPRESENTS THE EARTH. EACH IS PLACED AT A SPECIFIC ANGLE FROM THE VERTICAL.

TACK WELL, SEW BETTER

I n dressmaking, and other sorts of sewing, tacking, also known as basting, keeps the fabric in place before seams are stitched together permanently. Accurate tacking is always vital to the fit and finish of a garment.

After pieces of fabric have been pinned together the best tacking is done by hand, using a thread of contrasting colour so that it is easy to see when removing it. The ideal way to tack is to knot the thread at one end, and to make long stitches, bringing the needle out each time $^1/_4-^1/_2$in (6–12mm) beyond the place where it was inserted. For permanent stiffening, dressmakers of the past would tack whalebones into the seams before the final stitching was done.

Machine sewing then holds fabric pieces firmly in place. The earliest machines, like that invented for sewing leather by the Englishman Thomas Saint in 1790, created chain stitches, which easily unravelled if the thread snapped. The breakthrough came with lockstitch, made with one thread above and one below the fabric. The lockstitch

Before – and long after – the invention of the sewing machine, hand sewing was a social occupation. Women would take their needlework when visiting friends and neighbours and the 'sewing bee' existed as much for exchanging information, gossip and for story telling, as for stitching.

machine was invented in 1834 by Walter Hunt, but not patented until 1846 by the Massachusetts mechanic Elias Howe. In 1851 another American, Isaac Singer, made his own version, and although successfully sued by Howe for the patent, subsequently joined forces with him.

FIT A CANDLE TO A CANDLESTICK: DIP IT IN HOT WATER

The simplest and easiest way to soften the wax and allow a good fit, it is also safer and more reliable than trying to melt the candle end with a lighted match.

Soft candlelight provides a subtle evening ambience, but is no longer a necessity in the home as it was before the advent of gas or electric lights. If a candle starts to burn blue it is said that a spirit has entered the house.

The first candles were made by immersing rushes or flax fibres in animal or fish fat (tallow). Even by the 1920s, when most towns and cities were lit by

Incidentally...

In the smart 19th-century home it was customary to cover a naked flame with a candleshade made from silk, vellum or parchment. But the American author Mary Gay Humphries remarked: 'It is rarely that they do not topple over, set fire ... or by some mischance interrupt the progress of the dinner.'

electric light, country housewives still saved their kitchen 'scummings' for making tallow candles which, though economical, gave out a yellow light and an acrid smell. Beeswax candles came into use in the Middle Ages. They were pleasant smelling and produced a clear flame with no smoke, but they were very expensive.

Most candles are now made from paraffin wax and machine moulded. The best are made from spermaceti, the waxy substance found inside the head of a sperm whale.

A British Act of Parliament of 1860 defined a 'standard candle' as one made of spermaceti wax, six of which together weighed 1lb (450g), and which burnt 120 grains of wax an hour. From this specification came the original measures of gas and electric light in terms of candle power.

THE CHAMBERSTICK, WITH A DISH-LIKE BASE AND A CARRYING HANDLE, WAS THE CANDLE 'TO LIGHT YOU TO BED'. DESIGNED IN THE 17TH CENTURY, IT CHANGED LITTLE FOR ANOTHER 200 YEARS.

Candles improve with keeping. Left exposed to the air for a few months the wax hardens and will burn longer and brighter.

REMOVE WATER MARKS FROM FURNITURE WITH MAYONNAISE

This can work on light marks by drawing the water out of the wood, but the method is by no means infallible – even if, as some experts recommend, you mix in a little cigarette ash or toothpaste.

Even if it proves effective – and you need to rub the affected area gently for half an hour or more so that the oil in the mayonnaise can work into the wood, or leave the mixture in place for 12 hours before buffing – you may still have a problem. Because both ash and toothpaste are abrasive they can ruin the finish of the piece. A final, thorough waxing may help, but the bottom line is that water in any form, including wine, is bad for polished wood, and a valuable piece may need professional restoration.

Incidentally...

Heat can also damage wooden furniture. Placing a veneered piece next to a radiator can make it too warm and draw the natural moisture from the wood, causing the surface to rise up and cockle.

To prevent problems, protect your table with coasters. These were invented in the 1760s to avoid wine spillages on furniture and linens and were originally made from silver or Old Sheffield plate. They were not flat like modern coasters, but like shallow dishes, initially quite plain but by the early Victorian period intricately decorated.

COASTERS GET THEIR NAME FROM THE (MALE ONLY) AFTER-DINNER CUSTOM OF ROLLING BACK THE TABLECLOTH AND 'COASTING' – SLIDING – THE PORT, PLACED IN ITS SMOOTH-BOTTOMED CONTAINER, FROM DRINKER TO DRINKER.

TO GET YOUR WASHING WHITE, DRY IT IN THE SUN

Oxygen and ozone in the air work as bleaches that not only whiten but disinfect the wash – not to mention the added benefit of the wonderfully fresh aroma of sun-dried linens. On the downside, washing left outside is at the mercy of the weather.

If there is a light breeze, hanging the washing outdoors can also help remove creases from clothes and cut down on ironing. However, thick items like towels can get hard and stiff when dried in the sun, and may be better finished off in a tumble drier or airing cupboard.

There is an art to hanging out the washing. First you need to choose what to pin out: woollens, silks and delicate fabrics are better kept indoors and dried flat. It would have been second nature to the laundry maid to peg socks by the toes, shirts by the tails and dresses by the shoulders. Adjacent tea towels and handkerchiefs she would have pegged together at the corners, making a neat, firm row on the washing line.

For securing heavy or bulky items such as sheets and jeans so that they don't blow away there is still nothing to beat the traditional push-on American peg, or clothes pin, made from a single piece of wood. This is not only durable but, unlike the spring-grip peg (which comes in plastic as well as wood and is most suitable for more delicate items), has no metal to rust and mark the washing. The gypsy peg, rarely seen nowadays, is made from two pieces of whittled wood held together at one end with a band of metal.

Incidentally...

In seafaring communities, wives will never wash clothes on the day their menfolk set sail, for fear that this will, it is said, wash their ships away.

CLEAN BOTTLES WITH EGGSHELLS

When marks are inaccessible with a brush, crushed eggshells shaken inside a bottle or decanter with warm water and a little washing-up liquid make an excellent and effective cleaner.

Alternatively, you can buy boxes of 'magic' metal balls that do the same job by abrading the inside of the bottle. These are the modern version of the lead shot that butlers traditionally used in decanters, with the addition of brandy. Coal ashes shaken with hot or cold water are another old-fashioned cleaner.

Incidentally...

The shell of a hen's egg is 95 per cent calcium carbonate and is secreted around the yolk and white by the hen's shell gland, in a process that takes about 14 hours to complete.

It is traditional chicken-farming practice to add crushed eggshells to the birds' feed to provide the minerals they need to make fresh shells.

Eggshells have other good uses. Crushed and spread in the garden they can help to keep slugs and snails off your most vulnerable plants. In the kitchen, eggshells, well washed and crushed, can be used to clarify consommés; the cloudy particles in the liquid cling to the shells, which can then be filtered out.

SINCE THE 18TH CENTURY WINE BOTTLES HAVE BEEN MOULDED INTO IDENTIFIABLE SHAPES FOR SPECIFIC WINE REGIONS AND GRAPES, FROM THE 'SHOULDERED' BORDEAUX BOTTLE TO THE SQUAT, ROUND CHIANTI CONTAINER.

PUT WHITE WINE ON A RED WINE STAIN

Red wine spilt on a pale carpet or favourite sweater is the accident everyone dreads, but white wine is better drunk than wasted on a stain! Salt may work to a degree (and is good for bloodstains) but a mild detergent is by far the best.

When poured on to a stain, the bubbles in soda water can help lift a red wine stain from carpet or fabric fibres, but whatever remedy you choose, haste and a gentle touch are essential. Your aim should be to prevent the stain from 'setting', spreading or being rubbed into the fibres. The advantage of the detergent

approach is that you can whiz up a foam which can then be palmed on to a carpet to work on the stain without getting the pile soaking wet. The residue can then be carefully removed with a clean cloth, without rubbing, and the area neutralized with a dilute solution of white (not wine or malt) vinegar.

Incidentally...

To remove wine stains from linen, common 19th-century advice was to hold it in milk 'while boiling on the fire'.

Other good tips for spills and stains

Coffee and tea – detergent followed by vinegar, as for red wine.

Chewing gum – put a bag of ice cubes on the offending area, or put a garment in the freezer for at least an hour, then scrape off the hardened gum.

Ink, oil-based paint, butter – commercial dry cleaning fluid, followed by dilute household ammonia.

Blood, egg, milk, chocolate – detergent in cold water (to avoid cooking the stain), then vinegar diluted in water.

THE GARDENER'S
FRIEND

Adam and Eve were given no specific advice on how to tend the Garden of Eden, the perfect paradise containing 'every kind of tree pleasing to the eye and good for food', but for gardeners of today as for those of the past, the ideals are a year-round abundance of colour, flowers and foliage and vigorous, plentiful crops. Although it is a place of hard physical labour, the garden remains a source of great pleasure.

Gardening lore has been passed down the generations ever since the ancient Egyptians cultivated exotic plants gathered from other parts of Africa as well as from Asia and Europe. Many early gardens were attached to temples or monasteries, and plants were grown both for their medicinal qualities and for food, as well as for making wine and other drinks, and for the delights of their texture, hue and scent.

The old sayings and tips that still work today betray lifetimes of gardening trial and error, and it is no accident that experienced gardeners are described as 'old' green fingers or green thumbs. Over the centuries gardeners (and farmers) have learned how to tame nature, breed and cultivate ever more exotic plants, and cope with the worst the weather has to offer.

Sow Broad Beans on Boxing Day

A catchy way of saying that broad beans (*Vicia faba*) can be successfully overwintered, although both modern seed producers — and their predecessors — recommend sowing in mid to late autumn while the soil is still warm. The earlier they are sown the less prone the young plants will be, it is said, to attack by blackfly.

Gardeners can choose between two types of broad beans: short-podded Windsor beans (probably the original ingredient of brown Windsor soup), with four large beans to a pod, and longpod varieties with up to eight beans per pod. To stop the seeds being eaten by mice, 19th-century gardeners would roll them in paraffin before planting.

Eating broad beans has long been associated with the mysterious, sudden onset of a rare but debilitating illness, and modern medicine has revealed the beans to be responsible for setting off attacks of what is, for this reason,

Incidentally...

*Broad beans 'nestling', as the children's song says, 'in their blankety bed' of white fluff have a taste like no other. For millennia, broad or field beans were a staple food of Europe, North Africa and Western Asia, and retained their popularity until haricot beans (*Phaseolus vulgaris) *began to be imported to Europe from the America in the 16th century.*

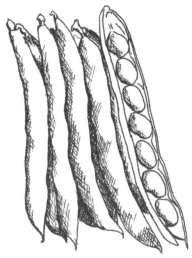

commonly known as favism. It is typified by headaches, blurred vision, dizziness and nausea — symptoms that come on within an hour or two of consumption. Favism is a hereditary condition, caused by the lack of an enzyme that is essential to broad bean metabolization, and resulting in the rapid destruction of red blood cells.

NEVER MOVE A PEONY

A peony will last a lifetime as long as you resist the temptation to move it from one bed to another. The tubers from which peonies grow are prized in legend for their healing powers and it is said that uprooting a peony will bring the worst of ill fortune.

Named after the Greek physician Paeon, peonies (*Paeonia* spp) have been cultivated since at least the 7th century, when the Chinese grew them for both their medicinal properties and their beauty. Today's gardener can choose from a huge range of species and varieties, from the sumptuous, ruffled double pink *P. lactiflora* 'Sarah Bernhardt' to *P. mlokosewitchii*, known colloquially as 'Molly the Witch', whose soft bluish foliage is topped with single lemon yellow flowers.

Incidentally…

The apothecary and gardener John Parkinson, writing in Theatrum Botanicum *in 1640 on cures for epilepsy, says: 'I saw a child freed from that disease, that had for eight whole months together, worn a good piece of the [peony] root about him.'*

Peonies need a fertile, well-composted soil and plenty of sunshine, though they are prone to damage by spring frosts if iced leaves are quickly warmed by bright sunshine. They arrived in Britain in profusion in the 1880s and their cultivation reached the height of fashion in Edwardian times. Favourites of the period were the large, often double-flowered, cultivars of *Paeonia lactiflora* imported from China and grown in preference to the 'ordinary' single-flowered European native, the red *P. officinalis*.

THE MOUTAN OR TREE PEONY (*P. SUFFRUTICOSA*), A NATIVE OF WESTERN CHINA, IS — AS ITS NAME SUGGESTS — A LARGE SHRUB, NOT A HERBACEOUS PERENNIAL. INTRODUCED TO JAPAN BY BUDDHIST MISSIONARIES IN THE 8TH CENTURY, IT HAS GIVEN RISE TO MANY HYBRIDS, BRED BOTH IN JAPAN AND IN THE WEST, WITH FINELY CUT FOLIAGE AND LARGE, DOUBLE FLOWERS IN COLOURS FROM WHITE AND PALE APRICOT TO DEEP CARMINE.

PROTECT NEWLY SOWN GRASS SEED WITH BLACK COTTON THREAD

With the addition of 'rag flutterers and rattles of tin and glass', as one 19th-century manual recommends, this is the tried and trusted way of scaring birds away from a lawn in the making, though not as quick and easy to put in place as today's birdproof netting or fleece.

The first lawns were probably medieval pleasure gardens planted with sweet-smelling herbs, but it was the Tudor love of ball games that gave birth to the quintessentially English lawn, which took shape from the greens and bowling alleys of the 16th century. Early lawns included daisies, violets and speedwell in profusion and only from the 18th century did the perfect greensward become the only acceptable foil for beds of flowers and shrubs.

Incidentally...

Except for perfectionists, lawn rolling is now confined to sports grounds; in 1863 the Journal of Horticulture *advised that 'mowing alone will not secure a good bottom without that compression which the roller... tends to give.'*

For the domestic garden, the Victorians favoured seeding over turfing, which gave patchy results at best. As now, all-purpose seed mixtures containing species such as rye grass (*Lolium perenne*), sheep's fescue (*Festuca ovina*) and meadow grass (*Poa pratensis*) were planted, but the lawn would also have contained clovers and trefoils. Pre-preparation was – and is – all-important, and it could take a whole year to clear the ground of weeds and stones and to plough, harrow and level it.

Lawns were cut with scythes until the lawn mower, first sold in 1832 by Ransomes, was invented by Edwin Budding, a Gloucestershire textile engineer. He based it on a machine he had devised for shearing the nap from velvet.

To KEEP HYDRANGEAS PINK, SPRINKLE THE SOIL WITH LIME

Pink is the natural colour of hydrangea flowers, but if you want to keep them that way you need to make sure the soil stays alkaline – which is why a dressing of lime does the trick.

Hydrangea flowers – nicknamed 'changeables' by the Victorians – are nature's soil indicators but are exact opposites to litmus paper. On acid soils the blooms will turn blue, but you can alter their colour artificially from pink to blue by adding aluminium sulphate to the soil or watering them with a bluing agent. Rusty nails or copper wire planted near the roots are effective old-fashioned bluing treatments.

Incidentally...

Hydrangeas get their name from the shape of their seed pods, which look like drinking cups. In Greek hydor *means water and* aggeion, *vessel.*

The flowers on a hydrangea head are of two kinds, the small fertile flowers and the showy sterile flowers, called ray florets. The mop-headed hortensias and the flat-headed lacecaps of *Hydrangea macrophylla* are the best-known sorts, but they like a protected position in the garden. *H. paniculata* 'Grandiflora' is a hardier choice for cold areas. For a more unusual look, search out elegant *H. aspera*, with soft felted leaves and large heads of fertile flowers bordered by just a few ray florets.

HYDRANGEAS ARE NATIVE TO ASIA AND THE AMERICAS AND WERE PROBABLY FIRST BROUGHT TO EUROPE BY THE GERMAN PLANT COLLECTOR ENGELBERT KAEMPFER, WHO SERVED IN JAPAN AS SURGEON TO THE DUTCH EAST INDIA COMPANY IN THE LATE 17TH AND EARLY 18TH CENTURIES.

DEADHEAD ROSES TO GET MORE FLOWERS

Large-flowered (hybrid tea) and cluster-flowered (floribunda) roses, when deadheaded, can be stimulated into producing a second flush of blooms. But don't deadhead species roses such as *Rosa rugosa* and *R. moyseii* or you'll miss their decorative autumn hips.

All roses put a great deal of their energy into making flowers and as much again into creating fruit after the blooms have faded. By removing dead heads you effectively allow the plant to make more flowers. Roses are best deadheaded with sharp secateurs, which prevent the stems from being ripped.

Roses also need careful attention well before they flower. A fungicide applied every two weeks from late winter, when the leaf buds are beginning to swell, will prevent black spot developing. Once the problem shows itself, usually in early summer, it is too late. Any infected leaves should be swept up and burnt in autumn.

Incidentally...

The Romans were obsessed with roses. The flowers and petals were thrown at public ceremonies and used for everything from garlands to pillow stuffings and love potions.

TO MAKE CELERY WHITE, EARTH IT UP

This was essential advice in the days before easy-to-grow self-blanching celery varieties were available. Even now, purists still prefer to grow trench celery and blanch it by submerging the stems in soil or wrapping them in cylinders of cardboard or newspaper tied in place with string.

Incidentally...

Celery gets its common name from Homer's reference in the Odyssey *to* selinon. *It is also called smallage — which derives from* ache, *its old French name. The scientific name,* Apium graveolens, *comes ultimately from the Celtic words for water (referring to celery's natural habitat) and 'strong smelling'.*

When daylight hits the cells of trench celery stems it stimulates chlorophyll production, which turns them green, and the purpose of burying or wrapping the stems is simply to stop the light getting in. Although this is time consuming — as is digging the trenches in the first instance — trench celery is more tolerant of frost than self-blanching sorts and even in hard winters can be left in the ground right through until spring. There are some old-fashioned pink and red varieties as well as white.

Over 3,000 years ago celery leaves were used by the ancient Egyptians, together with blue water lily petals, to make garlands that were placed in tombs. The Chinese grew a type of celery in the 5th century, but it had thin, strongly flavoured stems and was always cooked. By contrast the European version, whose cultivation was first recorded by the French horticulturalist Olivier de Serres in 1623, quickly became a popular raw salad ingredient.

NEVER PLANT CABBAGES IN THE SAME PLACE TWO YEARS RUNNING

Or any other brassicas – broccoli, cauliflowers or Brussels sprouts – for that matter. One of the good reasons for rotating garden crops is to help keep diseases at bay, including, for brassicas, debilitating club root.

Club root lives up to its name, swelling and distorting the roots of plants. This fungal disease, which is also sometimes called 'finger and toe', strikes during the growing season and severely hampers leaf production, resulting in leaves that are yellow and sickly, although they are still perfectly edible. There is no treatment other than to burn the affected plants. The best prevention is to treat the soil before planting with about 8oz hydrated lime per square yard (240g/sq m). The calcium in the lime is thought to deter fungal spores from germinating and penetrating the roots.

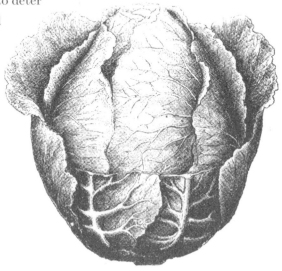

Incidentally…

The Romans ate large amounts of cabbage as a health food. And the latest research suggests that it may help to keep cancer at bay, especially colon cancer.

The theory behind the rotation of crops goes back to the three-field strip system of medieval farming. Each year one of the three fields was left unplanted (fallow) to allow it to recover its fertility. Four-field crop rotation was pioneered in the 18th century. Good composting and manuring makes a fallow period unnecessary in the average garden but good drainage, especially of clay soils, will always help vegetable health.

Deter slugs and snails with gravel

Every gardener has a favourite method of dealing with slugs and snails – from the chemical blast of pellets to wildlife-friendly methods such as surrounding plants with gravel to impede the pests' progress.

Since slugs can ravage beautiful young hostas, delphiniums or clematis overnight, not to mention destroying lettuces and other salad plants, and snails can even climb up raspberry canes to gorge on ripe fruit, it is hardly surprising that gardeners not only loathe these creatures with a passion but are forever searching for good methods of deterring or killing them. Some people swear

Incidentally...

A 'slugabed' is an Old English word for a lazy lie-abed. But a 'slughorn', originally a war-cry, has come to mean a battle trumpet.

that the only way to get rid of slugs and snails is to go out into the garden at night with a torch and pick them individually off the plants – and they do just that.

Slugs and snails are molluscs whose bodies consist largely of a muscular foot (which in snails curls up inside the shell when they are inactive or threatened). This not only secretes their tell-tale lubricating silvery trails, but contains organs of touch and smell powerful enough to detect potential food from a distance. Once a tasty vegetable meal has been located the creatures munch through it systematically using their sharp, file-like oral rasps.

Many suppliers advertise hostas that they claim are bred to have resistance to slugs, with variety names that include 'Big Daddy', 'Invincible' and 'Great Expectations', but they are unlikely to stave off attacks completely. The alternative solution is to choose plants that won't be eaten: for example, slugs really don't like the furry foliage of plants such as stachys.

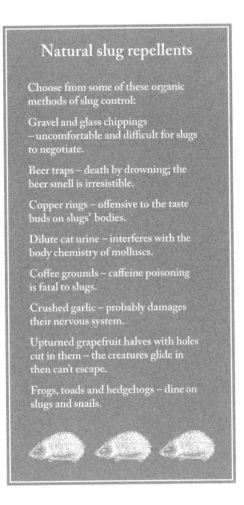

Natural slug repellents

Choose from some of these organic methods of slug control:

Gravel and glass chippings – uncomfortable and difficult for slugs to negotiate.

Beer traps – death by drowning; the beer smell is irresistible.

Copper rings – offensive to the taste buds on slugs' bodies.

Dilute cat urine – interferes with the body chemistry of molluscs.

Coffee grounds – caffeine poisoning is fatal to slugs.

Crushed garlic – probably damages their nervous system.

Upturned grapefruit halves with holes cut in them – the creatures glide in then can't escape.

Frogs, toads and hedgehogs – dine on slugs and snails.

IT IS SAID THAT IF YOU PLACE A SNAIL OVERNIGHT IN A DARK BOX ITS TRAIL WILL SPELL OUT THE INITIAL OF YOUR FUTURE SPOUSE.

IMPROVE THE SOIL BY DIGGING IN NEWSPAPERS

A good, eco-friendly low-cost ruse for adding 'structure' to light, chalky or sandy soil, though you will also need to add plenty of compost to boost soil nutrients. Water-absorbent low-quality paper (whatever the editorial style) rots down fastest.

The problem on fine soils is that the water drains from them too quickly, leaving plant roots dehydrated and leaching out nutrients. Apart from newspapers, which need to be finely shredded to speed rotting (there is no evidence that the ink has any ill effects on plants), try adding beached seaweed, if you can get it legally and are sure it is uncontaminated. Well washed to rid it of salt, which is lethal to plants in large quantities, seaweed rots quickly and adds potassium and iodine. On light soils, the sticky alginates it contains help bind soil particles together.

Incidentally...

The soil in gardens and farms comes from the broken, decayed rocks on the surface of the earth's crust, mixed with the rotted remains of plants and animals. The topsoil layer in a garden is usually little more than 4ft (1.2m) thick at most. Below this is the infertile subsoil.

Clay soils have the opposite problem. Their fine particles stick together tightly, making them rock hard when dry so that they impede drainage. For these, shredded paper plus grit, sharp sand (not builder's sand which is too fine and likely to be full of lime), fine gravel or pea shingle all work well as improvers. They need to be added at about 1½ spade depths, with a layer of well rotted manure placed on top.

> That clay bakes hard in the sun – and even harder when heated in a fire – is the logic behind pottery making, a craft with a history of at least 25,000 years.

LADYBIRDS ARE THE GARDENER'S FRIENDS

The ladybird or ladybug is our ally because both adults and larvae, also known as 'garden crocodiles', are voracious devourers of both aphids and the scale insects that attack garden flowers and crops.

Ladybirds (members of the insect family Coccinellidae) are small-winged, spotted beetles, usually coloured in a combination of either red or yellow with black. An individual can eat up to 150 aphids in a day. The eggs, mostly laid on the undersides of leaves, hatch into elongated larvae, dark grey with coloured blotches. These consume many times their own weight in other insects and their eggs. After shedding their external 'skin' several times they turn into the spherical pupae from which adults hatch.

The ladybird or 'beetle of our lady' got its name from its dedication to the Virgin Mary in the Middle Ages. The children's rhyme 'Ladybird, ladybird fly away home/Your house is on fire and your children will burn' is said to come from the burning of the hop fields in England at the end of the harvest, which destroyed many of these insects. But as well as flying away when disturbed, ladybirds will lie on their backs and 'play possum'. To make themselves unappetizing to bird predators they also exude blobs of pungent yellow 'blood'.

The Australian ladybird or vedalia beetle (*Rhodolia cardinalis*) was taken to Pacific North America in 1888, where it successfully eradicated the devastating cottony cushion scale from orange and lemon orchids.

THE MOST COMMON EUROPEAN LADYBIRD IS THE RED SEVEN-SPOT *COCCINELLA 7-PUNCTATA*. THE YELLOW *THEA 22-PUNCTATA* HAS 22 BLACK SPOTS, AS ITS NAME SUGGESTS. LESS WELCOME IS THE HARLEQUIN LADYBIRD (*HARMONIA AXYRIDIS*), THE MOST INVASIVE LADYBIRD ON EARTH, NAMED FOR ITS VARIABLE APPEARANCE, WHICH PREYS ON OTHER LADYBIRDS WHEN APHIDS ARE SCARCE. IT WAS INTRODUCED FROM ASIA TO NORTH AMERICA IN 1988, AND ARRIVED IN BRITAIN IN 2004.

STOP PICKING ASPARAGUS ON THE LONGEST DAY

The logic behind this good advice is to give the asparagus plants plenty of time to renew their underground resources before the onset of winter. Quite by chance, the longest day of the year coincides with the end of the six-week cropping season for English asparagus.

Asparagus is easy to grow as long as you have the patience to wait for the crowns to mature, since even if you plant three-year-old crowns (roots) the spears should not be cut for two years. But given good drainage, fertile soil and an annual top dressing of compost, a healthy bed can last for two decades and more. Growers of the past would bury animal horns, especially those of sheep, to help keep their asparagus beds fertile.

Incidentally...

The American guru of polite behaviour, Emily Post, recommends in Etiquette *(1960) that although 'by reputation this is a finger food... the ungraceful appearance of a bent stalk of asparagus falling limply into someone's mouth and the fact that moisture is also likely to drip from the end have been the reasons that most fastidious people invariably eat it — at least in part — with the fork'.*

The asparagus plant is a kind of lily, probably cultivated since ancient Egyptian times. It was a favourite of the ancient Romans, and Pliny the Elder described asparagus grown in Ravenna as so large as to be 'three to the pound'. Though it makes no difference to the crop, male and female flowers are borne on different plants. Choosing all male plants will stop the spread of seedlings that can sprout in profusion from shed female berries.

The name 'sperage' was used in English in the 16th and 17th centuries, later changed to 'sparrow grass'. Market traders still know it as 'grass'.

IF YOUR WEEDS ARE NETTLES, YOUR SOIL IS RICH IN NITROGEN

True. Nettles and many other weeds are excellent indicators of the soil type you have in your garden, the improvement it needs and the plants that will thrive.

Since nettles mean nitrogen, they are a sign that your plot will be ideal for leafy vegetables like spinach that also need nitrogen to thrive, but may be less suitable for fruit trees because it can stimulate them to make too much leaf and too little blossom (and fruit).

To balance up the soil, treat it with potash which, on soil already rich in

Incidentally…

*To attract butterflies and moths, leave a patch of nettles in a wild garden area. The beautiful burnished brass moth (*Diachrysia chrysitis*) and small tortoiseshell butterfly (*Aglais urticae*) lay their eggs on nettle leaves, which are avidly devoured by the caterpillars.*

nitrogen, is best supplied as potassium sulphate. Phosphorus is the other essential element for fertility, ensuring good root and fruit formation. It is best applied to the soil as phosphates, either in quick-acting liquid form or as slow-release rock phosphate. Good organic sources are farmyard manure and bone meal.

THE YOUNG LEAVES OF NETTLES HAVE LONG BEEN USED TO MAKE AN IRON-RICH HERBAL TEA BUT THEY SHOULD BE PICKED BEFORE MAY DAY. AFTER THAT, SO LEGEND HAS IT, THE DEVIL USES THEM TO MAKE HIS SHIRTS.

Soil signs

Look out for all these good soil indicators:

Nitrogen rich – stinging nettles (*Urtica dioica*), black nightshade (*Solanum nigrum*)

Lime rich – bindweed (*Convolvulus arvensis*)

Lime deficient – chamomile *Chamaemelum nobile*)

Loam – tansy (*Tanacetum vulgare*), dandelions (*Taraxacum* **spp**)

Clay – coltsfoot (*Tussilago farfara*)

Transplant
WHEN IT'S RAINING

O r, if you don't want to get soaked through, when the ground is nicely moist but not waterlogged. Your aim is to minimize the shock to plants of being moved and to prevent roots from drying out.

As it says in the gardening manuals, seedlings need to be transplanted when 'large enough to handle', but you need to water them well before you start. If the plants are packed close together, try easing them out of the soil with a small table fork.

What you want in your seedlings, apart from good leaf structure, is as much root as possible, for it is the roots that absorb water and nutrients from the soil and get the plants going.

Make planting holes for the transplants with a dibber or pointed trowel and add water to each hole unless the soil is already very wet.

Incidentally...

Trees and shrubs are best moved in autumn when they are dormant, and a rainy day is perfect to prevent dehydration. Should the roots become severed, cut back the branches of the tree accordingly, to even up the needs of the leaves with the water and nutrients that the roots are able to absorb.

Pop in the plants and firm them in gently to avoid damaging the roots. The exception are brassicas, which like their roots firmly embedded; tall ones like Brussels sprouts will rock about in the wind and fail to thrive if loosely planted. After transplanting the plants may flop a bit, but will almost certainly revive.

Some plants hate being moved and are always best sown in situ and thinned as they grow. Parsnips and pak choi, if they do not die when transplanted, will make poor growth. Primroses and peonies (see p 71) prefer not to be moved.

BEANS AND PEAS NOURISH THE SOIL

This is true up to a point but these crops, which have long associations with good fortune, also feed hungrily from the soil throughout their growing season.

Beans, peas and other leguminous plants have earned their soil-improving reputation from the fact that they can 'fix' nitrogen

FRENCH BEANS GET THEIR NAME FROM THE COUNTRY WHERE THEY ARE TRADITIONALLY MOST POPULAR, THOUGH IN FACT THEY ARE NATIVE TO SOUTH AMERICA, PROBABLY PERU.

from the air and use it to help their growth. They do this by virtue of the small white nodules on their roots. These are packed with nitrogen-grabbing bacteria of the genus *Rhizobium*, which 'infect' the roots of the young plants, making them — and their decorative relatives such as lupins and brooms — able to thrive on soil that is low in nitrogen.

Despite their ability to make use of nitrogen from the air — they rarely suffer from the leaf-yellowing typical of nitrogen deficiency — beans and peas also need plenty of phosphorus and potassium, the two essential elements represented respectively by the chemical symbols **P** and **K** in an **NPK** fertilizer. These are easily supplied in well-rotted compost and other organic mixtures such as blood and bone meal. For tenderness, legumes also like good drainage for, as the old saying goes, 'Sow beans in mud and they'll grow like wood.'

A POD WITH NINE PERFECT PEAS INSIDE IS AN OLD SIGN OF GOOD LUCK. IF AN UNMARRIED GIRL HANGS THE EMPTY POD ON THE LINTEL OF THE DOOR, THE FIRST MAN TO CROSS THE THRESHOLD WILL BE HER FUTURE HUSBAND.

DON'T PICK BRUSSELS SPROUTS UNTIL THEY'VE HAD A FROST ON THEM

This is a neat way of saying that most maincrop varieties of this winter vegetable won't be ready to pick until late autumn after the first frosts, though it is possible to plant earlier croppers. However, very cold weather makes even the hardiest varieties mushy and inedible when they thaw out.

Brussels sprouts (*Brassica oleracea*) are not difficult to grow as long as you have fertile, well-manured soil, ideally improved with lime, and enough space to accommodate them. Plants need to be set at least 2ft (60cm) apart in each direction and placed firmly in the soil in spring to prevent root sway (see transplanting, p 88). They also need protection from pigeons; fine netting has the added advantage of deterring cabbage white butterflies

Incidentally...

It is assumed (though not known for certain) that Brussels sprouts originated in Belgium as a rather odd kind of cabbage with miniatures growing up its stem. The first reliable references to sprouts in English and French cooking are from the 18th century, while in the USA Thomas Jefferson definitely planted them in his garden at Monticello in Virginia in 1812.

from laying their eggs on the leaves, which later hatch into hungry caterpillars.

For a good all-purpose variety choose an F1 hybrid such as 'Breeze', which has smooth, dark green buttons and is a vigorous grower. Of the early hybrids 'Peer Gynt' is a reliable selection. For sprouts with a difference grow a red variety such as 'Red Bull', whose colour intensifies as the weather grows colder.

BRUSSELS SPROUTS ARE A VEGETABLE PARTICULARLY HATED BY CHILDREN (AND MANY ADULTS) FOR THEIR STRONG, SLIGHTLY SULPHUROUS TASTE, ESPECIALLY WHEN OVERCOOKED. THEY HAVE A SURPRISINGLY DIFFERENT, NUTTY FLAVOUR WHEN THEY ARE FINELY SLICED RAW IN A SALAD WITH GRATED CARROTS, APPLES AND A MAYONNAISE DRESSING.

DON'T LET RASPBERRIES FRUIT IN THEIR FIRST YEAR

This is wise advice if you're growing summer-fruiting raspberries, which appreciate time to make good root systems before putting their energies into making fruit, but it's not necessary for late cropping varieties planted the previous autumn.

The secret of responding to raspberries' needs lies in the timing. Summer raspberries bear their fruits on shoots produced the previous year. Autumn ones make both shoots and fruits in the same year. Pruning the tops off summer raspberries in their first year encourages the plants to make strong, fruit-bearing shoots in their second. Plant care also depends on the season. The fruit-bearing stems of early raspberries should be cut back to a few inches

Incidentally...

The botanical name for the raspberry fruit is an etaerio, which describes a cluster of small, fleshy fruits (drupelets), each containing an individual stone or pip.

from the ground after the harvest is completed. By contrast all the stems of autumn-fruiting varieties need cutting back in late autumn or early spring, before the new season's shoots emerge. Leaving the tops on through the winter gives the plants some protection from frost.

Because they are shallow-rooted, all raspberries appreciate support, shelter and an absence of weeds, which suck vital water from the soil if left to grow. A mulch of bark, leaves or bracken, spread after the raspberries have been well watered, will help to conserve moisture and suppress most weeds, but it needs to be several inches thick to deter persistent perennial weeds such as convolvulus.

The raspberry gets the second part of its scientific name, *Rubus idaeus*, from the fact that (according to Pliny the Elder in the 1st century AD) it grew copiously on Mount Ida. According to legend the original raspberry was white but the nymph Ida, trying to calm the screams of the infant Jupiter, scratched her breast on the fruit she was picking for him and stained it red.

PLANT CROCUSES NEAR A LAVENDER HEDGE

T he smell of the lavender is believed to help deter birds, especially sparrows, from pecking crocuses to pieces, though in late winter when food is scarce this is unlikely to put off a hungry bird.

The attraction of crocuses is probably the vitamin and energy-rich pollen in the brightly coloured centres. Sparrows will also peck away at primroses when they too come into flower. Another good deterrent is to plant a dense carpet of corms – the underground

Incidentally...

It takes the stigmas from some 4,500 flowers to make just 1oz (28g) of saffron. The crocus stigmas are still picked laboriously by hand.

storage organs from which crocuses grow — so that any damage will be easily disguised, and to stagger the flowering season with a range of varieties, including autumn crocuses. There are dozens of shades of yellow, white and purple flowers to choose from, with showy stigmas and stamens in yellow, orange and deep red.

The stigmas of the autumn crocus (*Crocus sativus*) are the source of saffron, used in cooking for its colour and spicy, bitter flavour, and as a dye. The town of Saffron Walden in Essex is named from the once-prolific cultivation of the plant in these parts.

The Moghuls are thought to have introduced saffron to India and Persia before the 3rd century BC. Though introduced to Britain by the Romans, its cultivation died out until, in the 14th century, a pilgrim returning from the Holy Land is purported to have smuggled home a single precious corm in his staff — which he had hollowed out for the purpose.

Iran and Spain are now the largest producers of saffron. Don't confuse the saffron crocus with meadow saffron (*Colchicum autumnale*), which grows wild in Britain. This plant is poisonous in all its parts; it contains the toxic substance colchicine, which has been used as a remedy for gout since ancient times.

Good crocus choices for a long flowering season

Mid winter
C. *imperati* (dark and pale violet)

Late winter
C. *vernus* 'Remembrance' (dark violet),
C. *chrysanthus* 'Advance' (yellow)

Early spring
C. *sieberi* 'Albus' (white),
C. *tommasinianus* (pale lilac)

Early autumn
C. *banaticus* (lilac)

Mid autumn
C. *boryi* (white, purple veins),
C. *goulimyi* (pale lilac)

Late autumn
C. *cartwrightianus* (lilac, red stigmas)

NEVER GROW LABURNUM IN A GARDEN WHERE CHILDREN PLAY

L aburnum seeds, which look very like peas, are attractive to children but deadly poisonous. If you already have a laburnum growing in your garden, warn children to stay well away from the pods and seeds – and even the leaves which are also mildly toxic.

Its spring covering of long strings of yellow pea-like flowers gives the laburnum its common names of 'golden chain', 'golden rain' and 'watch and chain'. Within about five years the most popular garden variety, *Laburnum* x *watereri* 'Vossii' – which has the advantage of producing only a sparse number of seeds – will grow to a height of about 20ft (6m).

In the wild, the two species of laburnum *L. alpinum* and *L. anagyroides* ('Vossii' is a result of a cross between them) are found from France eastwards to Hungary. Both the wild species can be found in

Incidentally...

In a case of laburnum poisoning, don't try to make the victim vomit or administer an antidote. Call for medical help at once. If you think a dog has swallowed laburnum seeds, get it to the vet as quickly as you can.

British hedgerows, where they are thought to have been planted deliberately, possibly to attract honey bees but probably for their wood, which has long been prized for its unique grain pattern. Cut into thin strips it is traditionally incorporated into ornamental inlays and veneers. What is hard to fathom is that the trees are often found where sheep and cattle, which can also be poisoned by the seeds, are raised.

Other poisonous plants to grow with caution if you have children are foxgloves, yew, juniper and hellebores, which are all toxic if eaten. And beware of euphorbias, which (except for *E. pulcherrima*) exude a milky white sap that can severely irritate eyes and skin.

OLD-FASHIONED ANTIDOTES FOR LABURNUM POISONING WERE STRONG COFFEE AND SAL VOLATILE (AMMONIA).

ONE YEAR'S SEED, SEVEN YEARS' WEED

Not just an exhortation to get weeds out of the ground before they are mature enough to set seed, this saying is also testament to the quantity and longevity of the seeds that weed plants produce. Weed seeds are at their very worst, however, when they germinate into perennial pests that also multiply below ground.

Common annual weeds such as chickweed (*Stellaria media*), fat hen (*Chenopodium album*) and groundsel (*Senecio vulgaris*) are successful because they produce a profusion of seeds that germinate quickly and easily in any soil,

WEEDING IS A RELATIVELY MODERN CONCEPT. FAT HEN,
NOW A COMMON WEED IN VEGETABLE GARDENS AND
CULTIVATED FIELDS, THRIVES ON MANURED GROUND OF
ANY KIND AND WAS GATHERED AND EATEN IN PREHISTORIC
TIMES. AND UNTIL THE ELIZABETHAN ERA, NEARLY ALL
PLANTS WERE DEEMED TO HAVE A USE OF SOME KIND
– EITHER AS FOOD, MEDICINE OR COSMETICS.

maturing to make yet more seeds which, unlike many others, do not
need months of dormancy before bursting into life again. They are
hardy, too, often flourishing through the winter. Other seeds,
like those of the field poppy (*Papaver rhoeas*), produced by
the thousand in a single head, will lie dormant for years
until the soil is disturbed, as happened during World
War I on the battlefields of Flanders.

But annual weeds – especially if hoed from
your beds before they set seed – are relatively
easy to eradicate compared with perennials.
With bindweed (*Convolvulus arvensis*), creeping
buttercups (*Ranunculus repens*), horsetails
(*Equisetum arvense*) and their like, dogged
persistence, if not chemical warfare, is the
only way to stop your valuable plants from
getting choked.

Iron draw hoes, used in a 'towards the body' action,
were employed by the ancient Egyptians and the
Romans but these early hoes usually had short,
not long, handles. The first known hoes, used in
Mesopotamia in about 4000 BC, had flint 'blades'.

In October, manure your field, and your land its wealth shall yield

O r your garden, especially the vegetable plot. Manuring in autumn gives the compost time to break down over the winter, before seeds are planted in the spring. But if there is a very wet winter the rain may leech much of the goodness from the manure, so you may need to add fertilizer before planting.

You can buy compost or make your own, depending on convenience and the size of your plot. Well-rotted farmyard or stable manure is always good if you can get it, particularly if you need to improve the quality of light or clay soil, as it adds bulk as well as nutrients. For a smaller plot, bags of concentrated manure are a good alternative, though they lack bulk.

It is easy enough to make your own compost, but it is wise to rot fallen leaves separately as they can take several years to break down. Keep your compost heap well watered, especially in dry weather, and aerate it regularly by turning the material to speed decomposition. Adding a commercial compost accelerator is also helpful.

Incidentally…

In the days of the horse and cart children were routinely sent out into the street with shovels and buckets to gather fresh, steaming 'muck' for the garden – especially the rhubarb patch.

Add these to a compost heap

Annual weeds

Lawn mowings

Vegetable peelings, eggshells

Shredded newspaper

Coffee grounds and tea leaves

Healthy withered leaves, prunings, rhubarb leaves

Avoid

Perennial weeds

Fallen leaves

Meat and bones (can attract vermin)

Glossy magazine pages, cardboard

Banana peel (slow to rot)

Diseased stems, roots, leaves and fruit

Add compost to the soil when you double dig – put it in the lower part of the trench – or add it as a top dressing. You will be surprised how quickly earthworms will pull the compost downwards. and mix it into the soil.

KITCHEN WASTE WILL BREAK DOWN EVEN MORE QUICKLY IN A WORMERY IN WHICH BRANDLINGS (*EISENIA FOETIDA*) ARE ENCOURAGED TO BREED. YOU CAN BUY A 'STARTER' SET OF WORMS FROM A FISHING TACKLE SHOP THAT SELLS LIVE BAIT.

WHITEWASH YOUR GREENHOUSE IN SUMMER

O r, even better, once the weather starts warming up in late spring, to protect plants from the scorching effects of the sun. Before painted-on shading became popular, greenhouses were fitted on the outsides of their roofs with adjustable wooden blinds.

Incidentally...

Large, decorative glasshouses to enclose vines and peaches were commonplace in the Victorian gardens of the well-to-do. Usually built as handsome lean-tos, they were equipped with heating, run in hot water pipes from the house.

What you need for this job is proprietary water-soluble white shading or limewash, not the sort of whitewash you would use indoors for your walls. Ideally it needs to be brushed on in late spring and sponged off again in autumn. As well as shading, the plants in the summer greenhouse need to be well watered and given plenty of ventilation. These two tasks can now easily be automated. Ventilator mechanisms work by means of expanding latches, which open the greenhouse windows when heated.

In hot weather greenhouse plants appreciate extra humidity. You can supply this by spraying the greenhouse benches with water. Another idea is to hang up a towel with its end in a bowl of water which will be absorbed, then evaporate.

One of the most famous glasshouses ever built was the lily house at Chatsworth in Derbyshire, made for the Duke of Devonshire in the 1840s by Joseph Paxton. Its design was based on the natural ribbing in the leaf of the giant Victoria waterlily. Paxton went on to use the same principles in the construction of the Crystal Palace for the Great Exhibition held in London in 1851.

WATER PLANTS WELL OR NOT AT ALL

This is good advice, because just a little water will dampen only the top layer of soil and can encourage plants to develop roots near the surface. Too many of these shallow roots will make the plants liable to wind damage and render them unable to absorb sufficient nutrients from the soil.

The roots of a plant will extend healthily downwards (influenced by gravity) and outwards in their search for water, and a good soaking once a week will usually suffice, especially if your soil has been improved with water-retaining compost (see p 99). As you water, be sure to direct moisture to the roots of plants, not on to their leaves. This is not just economical but helps to prevent water drops from acting as miniature lenses, which in summer can concentrate the sun's rays and mar foliage with unsightly scorch marks.

Water seedlings and small plants carefully. All but the finest water spray can damage or even uproot them. For thirsty plants such as cucumbers

Incidentally...

Early watering cans did not have spouts. Vase-shaped clay pots perforated with holes in the base, which were made from the 1470s onwards, were simply held over thirsty plants. At that time gardeners also used hoses made of fabric.

and tomatoes, sink a terracotta flower pot or an inverted plastic bottle with its bottom cut off next to each one. You can then pour water into the receptacle and be sure that it is all going directly to the roots rather than evaporating from the soil surface.

Time of day is important. Evening watering is best in summer, to minimize evaporation. When the weather is cooler it is best to water in the morning, as this prevents it from freezing overnight and damaging plants.

PREVENT CONTAINER PLANTS FROM BECOMING WATERLOGGED BY PUTTING IN PLENTY OF DRAINAGE MATERIAL SUCH AS BROKEN PIECES OF TERRACOTTA OR POLYSTYRENE CHIPS BEFORE YOU ADD SOIL.

PLANT VEGETABLES WITH EDIBLE LEAVES WHEN THE MOON IS WANING

According to one piece of ancient lore this moon-based timing will stop the plants becoming full of sap and consequently running quickly to seed. By contrast, it is said, plants with edible roots, which need to be juicy, should be planted when the moon is waxing. Only trial and error can prove or disprove either saying.

Other lunar gardening tips

Plant nothing on the day of a new or full moon.

Gather mushrooms when the moon is young and rising.

Weed by moonlight – the shadow of your hoe will stop the weeds growing again.

Prune fruit trees in spring when the moon is waxing and they will not be damaged by frost.

To encourage your lawn to grow fast, cut it during the first quarter of the moon.

Most popular lunar gardening advice, however, totally contradicts these maxims, recommending that plants that produce their edible parts above ground should be sown or planted during the increasing light of the moon (from new to full) and those that produce food below ground should be sown or planted when the moon's light is decreasing night by night.

Probably since the establishment of the earliest human societies, the moon has influenced our behaviour. One of the earliest references linking gardening with the moon's phases was made by Pliny the Elder, who wrote in his *Natural History XVIII* in AD 77: 'All vegetable productions are cut, gathered, and housed to more advantage while the moon is on the wane,' and 'It is generally recommended… to make seed-plots when the moon is above the horizon.'

Incidentally…

For farmers of the past it was believed to be important for pigs and sheep to be killed on a waxing moon. A waning one would, they thought, make the flesh shrink. Equally, foals sired on the wane were thought liable to lack health and vigour.

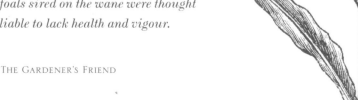

DON'T TREAD ON WET SOIL

It will become compacted and lack the essential air that plant roots need in order to grow. But use your feet to good effect – and with care – to firm in plants like shrubs when you plant them out.

There are lots of ways to avoid the problem. You can spread your weight by walking on planks or buy a roll-up plastic path especially designed for the purpose. In a vegetable garden, you can organize your plantings in slightly raised beds, each with a wooden surround. The trick is to make them narrow enough for you to reach the centre from either side without having to walk on them. It is also easy to cover beds like these with horticultural fleece in cold weather, making it possible to grow salad crops such as rocket all year round.

MIND WHERE YOU WALK ON THE LAWN, TOO, ESPECIALLY WHEN IT IS FROSTY. COMPACTING THE GRASS WITH ICE CAN LEAVE YOU WITH NASTY BARE PATCHES.

WHEN YOU PLANT FUCHSIAS, DIG IN CHOPPED BRACKEN

Bracken round the roots can help conserve the water that fuchsias like and it encourages their roots to grow strongly. In the winter, bracken fronds piled around and over fuchsia crowns can help protect plants from the frost to which even hardy varieties can be susceptible.

Incidentally...

*Fuchsias – originally garden escapes – are abundant in the hedgerows on the Isle of Man. The drop tree (*Fuchsia magellanica*) was first planted there, both in gardens and as hedging for farmland, in the 1830s, only about a decade after fuchsias were first introduced into Britain in 1823.*

The fuchsia, native to South America, the West Indies and New Zealand, is named for the 16th-century Bavarian botanist Leonart Fuchs and was first classified by the Swedish taxonomist Carolus Linnaeus in 1753. There are now endless varieties to choose from, ranging from vigorous, hardy shrubs with bright purple and scarlet flowers, such as *F. magellanica* 'Mrs Popple', to the subtle tones of the half-hardy trailing 'Pink Galore'.

Old carpet makes another useful soil covering and will suppress weeds. Put strips of it between rows of soft fruit such as raspberries and strawberries, which dislike weed interference.

In the autumn, bring half-hardy fuchsias into the greenhouse; keep them free of frost and watered just enough to stop them dying. Over-watering is likely to rot the roots. Hardy types can be left in situ in the garden, but cut the stems back to about 12in (30cm) from the ground. This will help to prevent the wind from rocking them and loosening the roots, while giving the plants some frost protection, which you can supplement with a covering of bracken or leaves.

BRACKEN (*PTERIDIUM AQUILINUM*) LOOKS WONDERFUL GROWING IN THE COUNTRYSIDE, ESPECIALLY WHEN IT TURNS YELLOW IN AUTUMN, BUT IS SO INVASIVE THAT IT CAN BE A MENACE IF IT GETS INTO THE GARDEN. IN COUNTRY AREAS IT HAS BEEN USED OVER THE YEARS FOR EVERYTHING FROM THATCHING TO ANIMAL BEDDING.

KITCHEN TIPS

As if by instinct, good cooks seem to know how to make everything turn out right. Their bread and cakes always rise, their sauces never curdle. As well as practice, the best cooks rely on the advice handed down by previous generations.

The oldest known recipes were inscribed on stone tablets in Mesopotamia in about 1700 BC. The only cookbook known from the classical world is that of Apicius from the 1st century AD, but the publishing of practical advice for home cooks really began in 1747 with *The Art of Cookery Made Plain and Easy* by the English author Hannah Glasse. The baton was taken up in Britain by Eliza Acton in her *Modern Cookery for Private Families* of 1845 and Isabella Beeton, whose *Book of Household Management* of 1861 remains a classic. But the American cook Fannie Merritt Farmer was determined to leave nothing to chance. As principal, she created *The Boston Cooking-School Cookbook* in 1896, with recipes measured accurately to the level teaspoon, tablespoon and cup.

Technology has transformed the kitchen since the days of the kitchen range, but however food is prepared, it is never more true than in cookery that practice makes perfect.

To save separated mayonnaise, add another egg

The 19th-century American perfectionist Fannie Merritt Farmer offered this sound advice, as have many good cooks before and since, though hot water is also recommended by some.

Mayonnaise, a fine emulsion of egg yolks and oil, is made by adding oil drop by drop to yolks mixed with some salt, while beating vigorously and continuously. What happens as you mix is that the oil is broken into smaller and smaller droplets, which eventually stabilize into a rich, thick mixture. Adding the oil too fast, or insufficient beating, are usually what makes the mixture separate out, so that pools of oil form, making the mixture look curdled. Keeping cool is, in every sense, critical to the process (and the sanity of the cook), because it makes everything more stable.

Incidentally...

Victorian cooks, who used mayonnaise to dress the salads then served for supper as main courses, rather than side dishes, dreaded having to make mayonnaise in hot weather, especially when it was thundery. For coloured mayonnaise, traditional additions were lobster coral for red, spinach or parsley for green.

'Smooth consistency,' says Miss Farmer, 'may be restored by taking the yolk of another egg and adding curdled mixture to it.' And she adds, 'It is desirable to have a bowl containing the mixture placed in a larger bowl of crushed ice, to which a small quantity of water has been added.'

WIPE, DON'T WASH, MUSHROOMS

The theory behind this age-old advice is that washing mushrooms makes them soggy, but since they are already 90 per cent water, a little more is not likely to make much difference.

The preparation method, therefore, is the cook's prerogative, though the tenacity with which pieces of dirt cling to the cups often makes washing the only practical cleaning method. Peeling today's cultivated mushrooms is almost always unnecessary, but may improve large field mushrooms that have

Incidentally...

Mushrooms have not always been appreciated or trusted. John Gerard, in his Herbal *of 1633, declared: 'Most of them do suffocate and strangle the eater,' while Nicholas Culpeper believed that 'Inwardly they are unwholesome, and unfit for the strongest constitutions.'*

Author Shirley Conran
introduced her 1975 bestseller
Superwoman with the motto:
'Life is too short to stuff
a mushroom.'

been gathered from the wild. When cooking
fine dishes the stalks of mushrooms are best
removed, and the frugal cook will keep them for
flavouring stocks or stews.

Most of the mushrooms we cook and eat
today are cultivated – and have been since the
17th century, when the French discovered how
to 'sow' the underground filaments or mycelia, from
which the mushrooms grow, in beds of asses' dung.

As palates become even more sophisticated, varieties of wild mushrooms
are becoming increasingly available, both fresh and dried, including caps
and chanterelles, both of which are especialy prized by the French. If you
live in the country, autumn is the time for mushroom hunting. As well as field
mushrooms, look out for edible parasols and puff balls, but also be sure to triple
check their identity in reliable books before you eat them.

Mushrooms were traditionally stewed with butter and served under roast
poultry or, in the 19th century, presented stuffed as an entrée. As a savoury
– a dish eaten at the end of an English dinner during the 19th and early 20th
centuries – mushrooms on toast was a popular choice.

IRISH FOLKLORE MAINTAINS THAT IF YOU SEE
A BUTTON MUSHROOM YOU SHOULD PLUCK
IT, AS IT WILL NOT GROW ANY MORE ONCE IT
HAS BEEN LOOKED AT.

NEVER COOK A GREEN POTATO

This is a case of 'green for danger', because the green colour betrays the presence of poisonous alkaloids. Similar substances are also found in other plants, ranging from nicotine in tobacco, caffeine in coffee and morphine in the juice of the opium poppy.

It is the same chemicals that give potatoes their great flavour that can also make them unsafe to eat. White potato flesh contains small amounts of the alkaloids solanine and chaconine, but when the tubers – especially small, young ones – are exposed to light, or are stored at too high or too low a temperature, alkaloid levels increase, producing green patches. Moreover, these chemicals are not destroyed by heat and, if eaten in quantity, create a burning sensation on the tongue, rather like pepper, which can be followed by collapse.

Incidentally...

Potatoes (Solanum tuberosum) *belong to the same plant family* (Solanaceae) *as the wild flower henbane* (Hyoscamus niger) *which contains the deadly alkaloids hyoscamine and hyoscine. These were used to murderous effect in 1910 by Dr Crippen to poison his wife.*

To be safe, a green potato should be discarded, although you may find that the green colouration extends only a little way beneath the skin. However, to get maximum nutrition from potatoes they are best cooked and eaten unpeeled. As well as the benefits of fibre in the outermost layer, most of the vitamin C potatoes contain is situated just beneath the skin, though contrary to popular belief the protein is well distributed throughout.

For the cook — and the gardener — the chief consideration in choosing potato varieties is whether they are waxy potatoes, which keep their shape when boiled, making them perfect for salads, or floury or 'mealy' potatoes, which are ideal for baking, mashing and frying.

> The potato was originally the staple food of the Incas of South America and has been in cultivation for at least 4,000 years.

STEW BOILED IS A STEW SPOILED

L ong and low is the cook's guide for guaranteeing tender meat in stews and casseroles. If the pot is allowed to boil hard the meat will become stringy, because the muscle fibres of which meat is composed shrink quickly, making them tough.

The stew has long been favoured by both busy and cost-conscious cooks. It can be left to simmer untended on a low heat, and this method of cooking can make even the most economical cuts of meat palatable. As the meat cooks, the tough collagen — the tissue that holds the bundles of muscle fibres together — is broken down into succulent gelatin. At the same time, the fat in the meat

Incidentally...

For a fish stew, like the flavoursome Mediterranean bouillabaisse, *gentle heat is needed not for tenderizing the ingredients but to make sure that the fish does not disintegrate into the cooking liquid.*

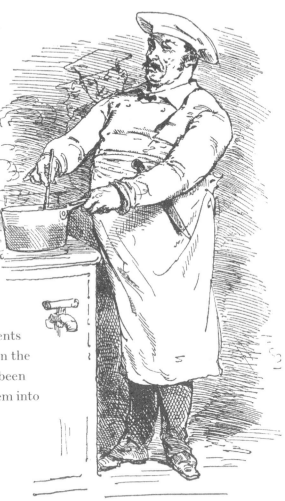

melts, deliciously infusing any potatoes or root vegetables added to the pot with its flavour.

Stews have their origins in the tradition of cooking over an open fire, the particular ingredients depending on local agriculture and climate. In an Irish stew, neck of mutton or kid are the key ingredients, plus potatoes, onions and a little water. No carrots, barley, leeks or other ingredients should, purists argue, be added, and when the stew is cooked all the liquid should have been absorbed by the potatoes, converting them into a thick, creamy mash.

THE CASSEROLE IS NAMED FOR THE POT IN WHICH IT IS COOKED: THIS WAS ORIGINALLY A FRENCH COPPER COOKING POT, OFTEN OSTENTATIOUSLY DISPLAYED ON THE WALL TO ADVERTISE THE WEALTH OF ITS OWNER RATHER THAN BEING USED ON THE STOVE.

HEAT A LEMON BEFORE YOU SQUEEZE IT

An old cook's tip made even easier if you have a microwave. Just 30 seconds on 'high' will soften the fruit's internal membranes. Five minutes in a warm oven works equally well.

Lemon juice is one of the cook's essential ingredients, for everything from a marinade to tenderize meat to a flavouring for a cake, so it makes sense to get every last drop of juice from the fruit.

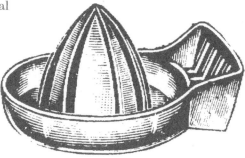

Incidentally...

Lemons were an expensive rarity until the 16th century, when the Italians began growing them in quantity and the Spanish planted the first lemon groves in California. Even when this rich lemon cheesecake recipe was written in the 1740s, in The Compleat Housewife *of Williamsburg, Virginia, lemons would still have been a luxury:*

   'Take two large lemons, grate off the peel of both and squeeze out the juice of one; add it to half a pound of fine sugar; twelve yolks of eggs, eight egg whites well beaten; then melt half a pound of butter in four or five spoonfuls of cream; then stir it all together, and set it over the fire, stirring 'till it be pretty thick... when 'tis cold, fill your patty-pans little more than half full; put a fine paste very thin at the bottom... half a hour, with a quick oven, will bake them.'

As well as applying gentle heat, another good way to help release maximum juice from a lemon (or a lime) is to roll it backwards and forwards on a work surface a few times before squeezing it.

Old-fashioned mechanical lemon squeezers come in two basic designs: the hand-held wooden 'reamer' and the glass pyramid moulded in a dish to catch the juice with protrusions to trap any pips and pulp. One ingenious 1930s device for extracting just a few drops of juice consisted of a perforated aluminium tube that was pushed into the lemon before the fruit was gently squeezed.

ALWAYS PEEL
ONIONS UNDER WATER

Immersion is good for two reasons. Peeling large onions in cold water can stop them making you cry. For small pickling onions and shallots, boiling water loosens the stubborn skins and eases peeling.

Peeling onions makes your eyes stream because they give off the volatile substances pyruvic acid and allicin (called lachrymators) when their tissues are cut. When these meet the fluid in the eye they create a weak – but stinging – solution. Under cold running water, the lachrymators have the chance of dissolving before they can get to the eyes. For slicing and chopping, however, there is no alternative to bearing the pain, but it may help to cool onions in the refrigerator before you cut them; this makes the lachrymators a little less volatile.

The fiery chemical components of onions are quickly and easily subdued by cooking. When heated, the volatile odours are dissipated; some are converted, for our pleasure, into sugar, others into chemicals more than 50 times sweeter. It is this sweetness that makes the tear-jerking preparation of a French onion soup or stew worthwhile, and onions so indispensable in the kitchen.

KEEPING CUT ONIONS IN THE HOUSE HAS LONG BEEN SAID TO BE UNLUCKY, BECAUSE IT WAS SAID THAT THE CUT SURFACE WOULD ABSORB IMPURITIES FROM THE AIR AND 'BREED DISTEMPERS'. ON THE OTHER HAND, A CUT ONION WAS SAID TO HAVE CURATIVE POWERS. WHEN PLACED IN A ROOM WITH A SICK CHILD IT WOULD, SOME BELIEVED, 'DRAW THE COMPLAINT TO ITSELF'. THE ONION WAS THEN SUMMARILY BURNT.

SALT SEASONS ALL THINGS

Not only savoury foods but sweet ones, such as cakes and pastries, need salt. The cook's essential for flavour has also been used for millennia as a food preservative.

No kitchen is complete without salt, simple sodium chloride, the white, crystalline chemical that comes from sea water and is also mined worldwide. As well as improving the taste of every savoury dish, a pinch of salt added to the flour in a cake or sweet pastry mixture improves the balance of flavours. When added to acid fruits such as pineapple and grapefruit, it even enhances their sweetness. Adjust the seasoning before you serve a dish but remember that many people are now deliberately lowering their sodium intake for health reasons. If in doubt, undersalt the dish and let guests add extra at the table. Don't forget that saltiness changes with temperature. A perfectly salted hot leek and potato soup will seem tasteless and bland when chilled and served as a vichyssoise.

Sea salt is the kind most prized by connoisseurs, especially when it has been made in the traditional way by evaporating sea water in the sun. Ordinary table salt is treated with small amounts of magnesium carbonate to keep it flowing freely. It may also be iodized – that is, have the mineral iodine added as a health benefit.

Preserving food by packing it in salt goes back to the Egyptian practice of salting fish in the 3rd millennium BC and this method became the norm in Iron Age Britain. The salt works by drawing out water, in which microbes flourish, and by killing any that do survive. By the Middle Ages, salt fish was Britain's standard fare. After salting, fish were also dried and smoked to become 'red herrings', which would keep undecayed for a whole year.

Salted foods

Many foods from around the world are traditionally preserved with salt:

Salt cod – the *fiel amigo* (faithful friend) of the Portuguese, is a traditional boon to Christians, who were banned from eating meat on Fridays and during fasting periods like Lent.

Sauerkraut – shredded cabbage layered with salt and fermented. It is associated with German cuisine, but was originally made by the Romans and Chinese.

Bacon – the original was Westphalian ham produced by Germanic tribes to preserve the meat of *Bachen* – wild pigs.

Salami – named from the Italian *salare*, meaning 'to salt'.

Salt pork – one of the basic winter provisions from Roman times onwards, it was for centuries a staple on board ship.

Soy sauce – salt is used in the fermentation of soya beans to make this signature of Asian cooking.

DON'T CHOP GARLIC WITH A KNIFE

Chopping garlic – or pressing it through a metal crusher – is the surest way to release the acrid chemicals it contains. A decisive bash with a wooden rolling pin or a swift crush beneath the flat of a knife blade is the best way to avoid the problem.

What happens when garlic is cut is that the enzyme allinase contained in its cells comes in contact and combines with a chemical called alliin to make allicin, one of the substances that make garlic smell. This quickly breaks down into the really acrid-smelling diallyl disulphide, the unmistakable garlic odour.

Avoiding garlic's acridity is especially important if it is to be used raw. For a fine dice, crush it first

Incidentally...

Garlic was once dubbed 'poor man's treacle' for its health-giving properties.
Modern medicine confirms that it helps to lower blood pressure and blood cholesterol, kills bacteria and viruses and acts as a nasal decongestant. It may even help to prevent cancer. However, Nicholas Culpeper advised strongly against eating too much garlic because it could create 'strange visions in the head'.

then chop it quickly. All garlic will, however, mellow on cooking. Roast garlic has a wonderfully mild flavour. Cut the top off whole heads, drizzle them with olive oil and sprinkle with sea salt. Bake them at 400°F/200°C/ Gas mark 6) for 45–60 minutes.

In Mediterranean cooking, garlic is the vital ingredient of the distinctive mayonnaise aïoli. In aïoli garni it is served with a mixture of hot, boiled ingredients including, by tradition, cod, snails, squid, fennel, onions and potatoes.

ALWAYS ADD SALT TO PORRIDGE

O f all the foods whose flavour is enhanced by salt, porridge comes top. But how much salt to add is a matter of taste. Purists insist on their morning booster being a savoury dish, not one sweetened with sugar or honey.

Though porridge is a general word for any 'mush' made with cereals such as oats or oatmeal, barley, rye, hominy or even polenta, it is the Scots who claim the dish – made with oats – as their own, and regard salt as a key ingredient. No self-respecting Scot, it is said, will allow any other addition but milk or cream. Sugar is strictly for children.

BY TRADITION, HIGHLAND SCOTS WOULD
SET PORRIDGE IN A MOULD – WHICH
WAS OFTEN A SIDEBOARD DRAWER – AND
CUT IT INTO CHUNKS, WHEN COLD, TO
TAKE OUT WITH THEM FOR SUSTENANCE
THROUGHOUT THE DAY.

Before the introduction of 'instant oats', porridge making was a ritual that demanded the use of a special stirrer known as a spurtle or 'porridge stick'. Water was put on to boil, oatmeal sprinkled in with the left hand and the porridge stirred with the right. In this, it is said, 'consists the art of porridge making, as on it being well done depends the absence of lumps or knots... Boil 10 minutes, then add salt and boil 10 minutes longer. It is best not to put the salt in till the end of 10 minutes as it has a tendency to harden the meal and prevent its fully expanding.'

Porridge is sustaining because oats have a low glycaemic index. This means that they are digested slowly, keeping blood sugar levels raised over a long period. This makes them an ideal food for endurance exercise, and porridge is the favoured breakfast of Britain's record-breaking long-distance runner Paula Radcliffe. Because they contain soluble fibre, oats can help lower your blood cholesterol level.

FOR PASTRY:
COOL WHILE MAKING, HOT WHILE BAKING

This is undoubtedly the key to success with everyday shortcrust or 'plain' pastry, and for flaky and puff pastry. The exceptions are fancy pastries such as choux and the hot water crust used for authentic pork and game pies.

In making shortcrust pastry, coolness is vital to prevent sticky gluten in the flour from developing and to keep the particles of fat (lard, butter or a mixture

Incidentally...

Puff pastry is made by folding pastry in layers, with butter added between each. Coolness is essential during its preparation, but the finished dough, composed of up to 240 layers, needs very high heat (420°F/220°C/Gas mark 7) to expand the air trapped in the layers as quickly as possible, and to make the pastry crisp and golden.

of the two) from becoming liquid and thus a less effective barrier between the grains of flour. To keep everything as cool as possible, use chilled fat, cut it into the flour with a knife, then rub it in with the fingertips. Quickly stir in chilled water with a knife, and finish the mixture using the fingers of one hand until it just leaves the sides of the bowl. Half an hour's rest in the refrigerator, followed by rolling of the dough with a marble or glass rolling pin on a cool worktop, are the other essentials for avoiding heat, though it is fine to use an old fashioned wooden rolling pin if you wish.

In a hot oven (400°F/200°C/Gas mark 6) the particles of fat or shortening melt but, because they have kept the flour grains separate, long strands of gluten are prevented from forming. Quick, high-temperature cooking also keeps the starch grains in the flour stiff, making the pastry crisp. This, combined with the expansion of air trapped in the mixture and the release of steam as the water in the mixture evaporates, gives the pastry its lightness.

SOME LARGE VICTORIAN KITCHENS HAD SEPARATE PASTRY ROOMS FITTED WITH COOL MARBLE TABLETOPS, WHICH WOULD HAVE BEEN A BOON TO COOKS IN THE SUMMER MONTHS.

WHEN MAKING TEA, ADD ONE FOR THE POT

Grandmother's dictum results in a good strong brew, but today it is a matter of taste. However you make it, 'a nice cup of tea' has undoubted health benefits. Tea is rich in antioxidants, substances that can help reduce the risk of heart disease. Green tea may also lower your risk of cancer, especially stomach cancer.

Though tea bags are hard to beat for convenience, the pure flavour of a high quality tea can be appreciated only by using leaf tea in a pot. When you pour boiling water on to a

Incidentally...

According to Chinese legend, in the year 2737 BC the Emperor Shen Nung was resting under a tea tree when the wind blew some leaves into some water he was heating. The resulting drink so refreshed and revitalized him that tea drinking was 'invented'.

black tea (very hot, not boiling, is best for green tea), it releases a variety of substances, including caffeine, essential oils, polyphenols and the tannins that give tea its astringent or tightening effect on the palate.

While some people insist that tea's flavour is best (and good manners best satisfied) when tea is put in the cup first, others maintain that it is only possibly to get the strength exactly right if it is added after the milk. The British, who began drinking tea in the 1650s (the merchant Thomas Garraway first sold it at his London store in 1658) were probably the first to add milk, to help soften tea's bitter tannins. Putting the milk in first may have helped to prevent fine Chinese porcelain tea bowls from cracking with the heat of the tea.

Perfect tea

There is little agreement on what makes a perfect cup of tea, but this is one highly recommended method:

1. Fill a kettle with freshly drawn water, filtered if high in calcium carbonate, and bring to the boil.

2. When the water is nearly boiling, pour a little into the pot, swirl around and discard.

3. Measure one teaspoon of tea per cup into the pot.

4. Take the teapot to the kettle and pour the boiling water on to the leaves. Put on the lid.

5. Allow to brew until the tea is as strong as you wish.

6. Strain into tea cups, then add milk and sugar to taste.

THE CHINESE ADAPTED THEIR STONEWARE WINE EWERS TO SERVE AS TEAPOTS, BUT TEAPOT DESIGN DID NOT REALLY TAKE OFF UNTIL THE DUTCH BEGAN IMPORTING TEA IN THE LATE 16TH CENTURY. EVEN THEN, IT TOOK UNTIL THE 1670S FOR DUTCH POTTERS TO MASTER THE ART OF MAKING HEATPROOF VESSELS.

STOP MILK BOILING OVER: GREASE THE TOP OF THE PAN WITH BUTTER

Or, even easier, add a large, clean marble, but the failsafe solution is to use a heavy pan on a low to moderate heat and to stir and keep watch over the milk as it warms up. The other advantage of a heavy pan is that it prevents heated milk sticking and burning.

Hot milk can boil over in a second, but caught at the instant when the froth is just rising it makes the perfect addition to hot chocolate. The grease trick works because it helps prevent the foam from rising up the pan, but only temporarily. The marble acts as an in-built stirrer, but it, too, is fallible. Frothing milk with a jet of steam – which is what the steamer nozzle on an espresso coffee

A NON-STICK PAN WON'T STOP MILK BOILING OVER BUT WILL MAKE CLEANING EASIER. TEFLON, ORIGINALLY PRODUCED IN THE USA BY THE DU PONT COMPANY IN 1938, WAS FIRST USED TO COAT PANS IN 1955 BY THE FRENCHMAN MARC GRÉGOIRE.

Incidentally...

In the days before every home had a refrigerator, boiling or scalding milk before it was drunk was a vital precaution against infection, especially in hot weather and for the sick. Fannie Merritt Farmer recommended scalding it in a double boiler until the milk around the edge has 'a bead-like appearance'.

machine achieves – is an ideal solution, and prevents unpalatable skin forming. When using a pan, stirring the milk helps, although stirring in a skin once it has formed merely spreads the unappetizing bits through the rest of the milk.

ALWAYS ADD VINEGAR TO THE WATER WHEN YOU POACH AN EGG

For the inexperienced cook, this is a sensible precaution, as it helps the egg white to seal quickly and prevents it breaking up in the water – lemon juice has the same effect. Too much vinegar can mar the flavour if the eggs are to be eaten plain, but will be thoroughly disguised by a sauce.

Making perfectly poached eggs is a culinary art worth mastering. Start with a deep frying pan filled with 3in (7.5cm) of water with, if you wish, 1–2 tablespoons of mild vinegar added. When the water has reached a rolling boil, crack an egg into a part of the water that is bubbling hard so that it spins around in the vortex. (If you are nervous, break the egg into a saucer first, then slide it into the water.) Add more eggs in the same way, then lower the heat to get the gentlest of simmers. In about four minutes the whites should be set and the yolks still runny. Lift out the cooked eggs with a slotted spoon and drain them. Trim away any untidy white around the edges before serving.

Eggs Benedict – English muffin topped with grilled Canadian bacon (not cold ham), poached eggs, hollandaise sauce and (for sheer luxury) a slice of truffle, has been an American favourite for decades. There are various versions of its origin. One is that Mrs LeGrand Benedict devised it, in conjunction with the chef at New York's Delmonico's Restaurant, in the 1860s. Another is that in 1894 it was ordered in the Waldorf Hotel by Lemuel Benedict, a Wall Street broker, when suffering from a hangover.

The fresher the eggs, the better the white of a poached egg will set, making a neat, plump cushion around the yolk. Never add salt to the poaching water as it will break up the white.

EAT OYSTERS ONLY WHEN THERE'S AN 'R' IN THE MONTH

This is a catchy way of warning against the possibility of food poisoning from oysters, mussels and other crustaceans in the warmest months (in the northern hemisphere) of May to August, none of which includes a letter 'r' in their name. Nowadays oysters are bred and farmed to reduce the risk of infection all year round, but in summer, when they are fertile, they have an inferior taste.

Oysters feed on microscopic algae, which can become infected with bacteria, and these multiply rapidly in warm sea water. Of these bacteria, *Vibrio parahaemolyticus* is the most common, causing stomach pains and sickness,

Incidentally...

The reputation of oysters as an aphrodisiac (the famed 18th-century Italian lover Casanova is said to have eaten 40 a day) may be justified by their mineral content as well as their looks and texture. They are rich in zinc, a substance essential to sperm production.

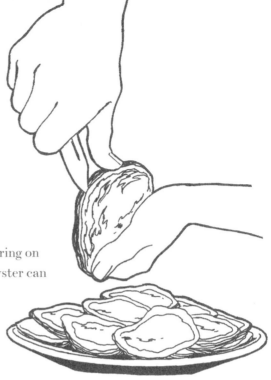

but most deadly is *V. vulnificus*, which can bring on septicaemia. What's more, eating one bad oyster can sensitize you to them all.

A 'good' oyster should always be tightly closed when you buy it and should open when it is cooked. If it is to be eaten raw, an oyster must be scrubbed clean then prized open with an oyster knife. Cooks would traditionally keep live oysters in the kitchen for a few days and feed them with oatmeal to fatten them and make them more luscious. The smallest of them were saved for eating raw, larger ones cooked and added to steak pies or turkey stuffing, made into patties or dipped in batter and fried.

Oysters were so abundant in Britain until the early 19th century that they were regarded as poor people's food. Sam Weller, in Charles Dickens' *Pickwick Papers*, declares that 'poverty and oysters always seem to go together'.

THE AMERICAN OYSTER DISH HANGTOWN FRY IS SAID TO HAVE BEEN THE FAVOURITE 'LAST BREAKFAST' OF THE CONDEMNED IN PLACERVILLE, CALIFORNIA, A SETTLEMENT THAT WAS NICKNAMED HANGTOWN IN 1849 FROM ITS OVERZEALOUS JUDGE. THE DISH IS AN OMELETTE MADE WITH OYSTERS DIPPED IN EGG AND FLOUR OR BREADCRUMBS AND FRIED.

YOU CAN'T MAKE BREAD IN A COLD KITCHEN

U nless, that is, you are making unleavened bread or soda
bread, which need no yeast. Warmth is essential to the
magic of bread making: it allows the live yeast cells to
multiply and, as they do so, produce the carbon dioxide gas that
makes the mixture rise.

Yeast (*Saccharoymyces cerevisiae*) is a single-celled fungus that is fussy about
warmth. Below 70°F (21°C) its cells reproduce only very slowly. Above about
130°F (56°C) they die. The temperature at which they grow fastest and
most steadily is just above human body
temperature, at 100°F (38°C). *Candida*
yeast, which produces the lactic acid
that gives sourdough bread
its characteristic flavour,
needs a similar
temperature.

Cooling bread is as important to perfection as cooking, because it ensures that water migrates to the crust and does not make the crumb doughy and leathery. Mrs Beeton advises strongly against eating newly cooked bread. 'It should,' she says, 'be carefully shunned by everybody who has the slightest respect for that much-injured individual – the Stomach.'

Incidentally...

The yeast used in bread making is the same live species (though today it is a different variety) as that used for making beer. The ancient Egyptians combined their breweries and bakehouses, using the waste or 'barm' from beer making to raise their bread. Women were responsible for both brewing and baking.

Steps in bread making the Mrs Beeton way

The domestic guru used 1oz (25g) fresh German (compressed) yeast for every 3½lb (1.6kg) flour.

1. Mix yeast with ¾ pint (450ml) of warm milk-and-water and mix until 'smooth as cream'.

2. Put the flour in a bowl with a pinch of salt and make a well in the middle. Pour in the yeast mixture and stir to make a 'thick batter in which there must be no lumps'.

3. Sprinkle plenty of flour on top and cover with a thick, clean cloth. 'Set it where the air is warm' but not 'upon the kitchen fender, for it will be too much heated there' until bubbles break through the flour.

4. Pour in a further ½ pint (300ml) warm milk-and-water. Throw on plenty of flour, then knead well 'with the knuckles of both hands' until the mixture is smooth. It is ready when it 'does not stick to the hands when touched'.

5. Leave to rise again, for ¾ hour. When it has risen and is beginning to crack, quickly cut into shapes and bake at once in a hot oven.

THE SEEMINGLY MIRACULOUS PROPERTIES OF YEAST LED TO ITS MEDIEVAL NAME OF 'GODDISGOODE' – BECAUSE IT WAS SAID TO HAVE COME FROM 'THE GREAT GRACE OF GOD'.

Don't open the oven door while a cake is cooking

Especially important for sponge cakes which, like soufflés, won't rise properly if subjected to a blast of cold air. For a perfect result the oven needs to be heated to the correct temperature before the cake is put inside.

A 'true' sponge cake rises because the air whisked into it expands in the heat of the oven. Classic whisked fatless sponges are the Savoy, in which egg yolks are first beaten with sugar, and the egg whites then beaten until stiff and folded in separately, and the Génoise, in which whole eggs are used. For both, the flour is folded in at the end of mixing.

Incidentally...

Until the gas cooker made its entry into kitchens from the 1890s cooks were at the mercy of the range, which, although it had ventilators to help control the fierceness and heat of the fire, was hit and miss for cake making. The manufacturers of gas cookers were quick to produce recipe books to accompany their stoves; the 1930s Parkinson Cookery Book *boasts that 'Cakes carefully prepared and put into a controlled oven heated to the correct temperature and given the right time cannot be failures.'*

In a creamed sponge, such as a Victoria sponge or sandwich cake, butter and caster sugar are creamed together until soft, then eggs, flour and baking powder are added. When heated, the flour produces pockets of carbon dioxide in the mixture. Both this gas, and the expanded, heated air beaten into the cake, will contract quickly if the oven door is opened and cold air rushes in.

FOR MAKING A VICTORIA SPONGE, THE CLASSIC PROPORTIONS ARE THE 'WEIGHT OF TWO EGGS' FOR EACH OF THE MAIN INGREDIENTS. SINCE AN EGG WEIGHS ABOUT 2OZ (50G), THE MIXTURE NEEDS 4OZ (100G) EACH OF SUGAR, BUTTER AND FLOUR. TO GET THESE PROPORTIONS EXACTLY RIGHT, MANY COOKS STILL PUT THE EGGS ON THEIR SCALES INSTEAD OF COUNTERBALANCING WEIGHTS.

FAT IS HOT ENOUGH FOR FRYING WHEN IT SMOKES

This old rule may work for lard but is more likely to ruin your cooking, for by the time they are smoking hot fats are not only beginning to burn but will also contain acrid chemicals that mar the taste of food.

When fats are heated they eventually reach their smoke point, which is generally a lower temperature for vegetable fats such as olive oil than it is for animal fats. The fumes they produce when they start to smoke contain the noxious substance acrolein and unpleasant-tasting free fatty acids. Butter that is heated to its smoke point is brown and burnt, well beyond the nutty brown stage called *beurre noisette*, which makes an ideal accompaniment to skate and other white fish.

Incidentally...

Deep frying is a perfect way of cooking foods that need to be sealed on the outside so that the water inside is converted to steam. This is what makes fritters and tempura so succulent. In shallow or pan frying, fierce heat at the start of cooking makes the outer most layer of meat brown and flavoursome.

A far better way of testing fat for deep (once also known as French) frying is to drop a piece of stale bread in the pan. If it browns in about a minute then the fat is hot enough. The same technique works for shallow frying, but when making pancakes use a teaspoon to add a few drops of batter to the pan. The fat is hot enough if the batter starts to set at once.

It's said that you can use taste alone to detect whether you're in the north of France or the south. Regional cuisines in the north use butter for cooking, those in the south favour olive oil.

THAT THE INSIDE OF THE FRYING PAN IS THE HOTTEST SPOT IN THE KITCHEN IS REFLECTED IN THE SAYING 'OUT OF THE FRYING-PAN, INTO THE FIRE'. BOTH ARE AS BAD AS EACH OTHER.

You can't overcook pork

In other words, make sure that the meat is really well cooked through. Historically, the reason for this caution was that 'measly' pig meat harboured the eggs of tapeworms. If these were not killed by heat, they could hatch out in the human intestine, with disastrous consequences to a person's health.

We can be more confident, today, that the pork we buy from the butcher or supermarket is safe to eat, but it has not always been so, especially in hot weather. In his *Shilling Cookery for the People* of 1860 Alexis Soyer recommended watching out for 'little kernels' in the fat – the tell-tale signs of measliness – and warned against 'clammy and moist' flesh. Rather than touching the meat he suggested poking it with a wooden skewer, then allowing the nose to test for freshness.

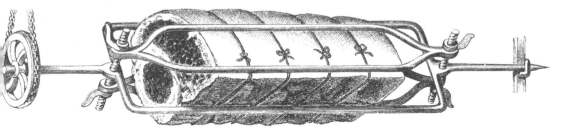

Incidentally...

The unfortunate pig has long held the reputation of being a lazy, gluttonous and unclean animal. Moses, as recorded in the Book of Leviticus, expressly forbade the Israelites from eating pork, declaring that, 'although it is a hoofed animal with cloven hoofs' the pig is unclean because 'it does not chew the cud'.

Apart from careful timing when roasting pork, the cook's challenge lies in getting good crackling, eulogized by Charles Lamb in his essays of the 1820s as 'a felicity… no pen can chronicle'. Opinions are divided as to the best technique for producing crackling. Some favour dredging the skin with flour, others advocate a mixture of salt and oil, yet others salt alone. Whichever method is used, deep fine scoring will help, as will allowing the skin to dry out thoroughly before roasting.

It is said that there is a use for every part of a pig – except the squeak.

PIGS, BEING VERSATILE, UNFUSSY FEEDERS AND EASY TO KEEP, WERE BRED FOR FOOD BY THE ANCIENT CHINESE IN THE 3RD CENTURY BC. IN MEDIEVAL WESTERN EUROPE PIGS LIVED ON 'PANNAGE' OR WILD FOOD, FORAGING IN WOODLAND FOR ACORNS AND BEECH MAST UNDER THE CARE OF A SWINEHERD. LATER, COTTAGERS KEPT ONE OR TWO PIGS IN A STY AND FED THEM ON HOUSEHOLD SCRAPS, BUT EVEN IN THE 19TH CENTURY THEY STILL ROAMED FREELY AROUND NEW YORK CITY, FORAGING IN THE STREETS FOR FOOD.

WHISK EGG WHITES IN A COPPER BOWL

For a stable foam that can be whisked stiff and will not collapse, there is nothing to surpass a copper bowl, but a clean, dry container, whatever it is made of, is essential to a good result.

Incidentally...

Dropping egg white into water (all of it, or a few drops from an egg pricked with a pin) and interpreting the shape created is an old method of divination. Gypsies are reported to have 'seen' everything from ships to churches and coffins using this method.

One of the problems of beating egg whites stiff, particularly for making meringues, is that if overbeaten they separate out into a nasty mess of lumps and liquid. What cooks of the past discovered by trial and error has now been proved in the laboratory: a reaction between conalbumin (one of the proteins in the white) and the copper prevents the foam from separating and imparts a creamy yellow colour quite different from the snowy white of a foam whisked in a glass, stainless steel or ceramic bowl.

Pure egg white is essential to a good result. Just a drop of yolk can reduce the volume of beaten egg white by over 60 per cent; particles of oil or grease can have a similar but less drastic effect. Salt makes whites hard to whip and decreases their stability. If you have a copper bowl, keep it spotless. Rub off any green patches of potentially harmful copper oxide with a mixture of salt and lemon juice, then wash and dry it thoroughly before use.

THE FIRST EGG WHISKS WERE BUNCHES OF BIRCH TWIGS, USED IN THE 16TH CENTURY TO MAKE 'SNOWS' OF BEATEN EGG WHITES AND CREAM — THE FORERUNNERS OF MERINGUES.

THE SHORTER THE FIBRES, THE MORE TENDER THE FLESH

A handy rule for judging the quality of the butcher's meat, though not the only important factor. The cut is critical as is, for beef especially, the length of time the meat has been hung.

Meat is muscle, made of bundles of long, thin fibres, which are supported by sheets of connective tissue containing collagen. Age and exercise toughen muscle fibres – by increasing the number of fibres in every muscle bundle – but with age also comes the deposition of fat, the 'marbling' that melts in cooking and adds to meat's succulence. Animal anatomy is also significant. The muscles of the forequarters, which the animal uses more, are

Incidentally...

In the 1940s two young entrepreneurs paid a small sum to a Californian restaurateur for his 'magic formula' – a substance for tenderizing cheap cuts of meat. So began the widescale sale of meat tenderizers based on the papaya enzyme, though for centuries before this the people of South and Central America had been improving their meat by wrapping it in papaya leaves.

generally tougher and more packed with collagen than those of the rump or those near the spine and under the backbone.

Cuts such as steaks combine the advantages of being from the rump of the animal and having short fibres. Slicing meat across the grain – as in a T-bone steak or meat sliced for a stroganoff or a Chinese stir fry – helps to create short fibres which, though probably already tender, are extremely easy to chew.

Tenderness also depends on an animal's health. A well-fed creature will have plump muscle fibres packed with the carbohydrate glycogen. In the carcass this is converted into lactic acid, which tenderizes the flesh by breaking down the protein in the muscle fibres and also helps to prevent it from being infected with bacteria.

With hanging, enzymes are released that both add acidity to the meat, enhancing its flavour, and improve its tenderness. You can judge a well-hung piece of beef by its deep – not bright – red colour. Beef can safely be hung for up to six or even eight weeks, though today's commercial pressures make three weeks the norm.

PRICK SAUSAGE SKINS TO STOP THEM BURSTING

Pricking is a useful precaution if sausages are not of the highest quality, and for any sausages to be cooked at high temperatures, but it allows the juices to leak from good sausages, reducing their succulence.

The more water there is in a sausage the more likely it is to burst when cooked. Sausages earned their nickname of 'bangers' when, during the 1940s, they were so packed with water that they were likely to explode when heated. Modern sausage makers recommend no pricking and slow frying or cooking under a moderate grill to stop the skins bursting. An old method of toughening sausage skins or casings — made from animal intestines or, as Fannie Merrit Farmer called them, 'prepared entrails' — was to dip the sausages in boiling water before they were cooked.

Many culinary regions have characteristic types of sausage that relate closely to the climate. So it is no accident that dried sausages that keep well, such as salami, came first from warm countries such as Italy and Spain. The frankfurter is named for Frankfurt am Main, but 'hot dog' entered the vocabulary when, in 1906, the American cartoonist Tad Dorgan depicted a sausage dog (a dachshund) served up in a bun.

The expression 'not a sausage', which when first coined meant lack of money, relates back to cockney rhyming slang in which bangers and mash equal cash.

A QUINTESSENTIALLY ENGLISH SAUSAGE DISH IS TOAD-IN-THE-HOLE, MADE FROM SAUSAGES BAKED IN YORKSHIRE PUDDING BATTER. DESCRIBED BY MRS BEETON AS 'HOMELY BUT SAVOURY' (SHE USED STEAK AND KIDNEY IN IT, NOT SAUSAGE), IT WAS FIRST MADE IN THE 18TH CENTURY.

DON'T STORE BANANAS IN THE FRIDGE

Because they are averse to cold. If you must refrigerate bananas, wrap them in newspaper to keep them insulated. Their skins may turn black but they should be prevented from going mushy inside.

If you want to eat or cook with bananas ripened to your taste it is best to buy them green and allow them to ripen slowly. Supermarket bananas are picked completely green and allowed to ripen somewhat during shipment. As they mature the starch in the flesh turns increasingly to the sugar glucose, which helps to alter the texture as well as the taste of the fruit.

When bananas are fully ripe – as you need them for mashing into a banana bread mixture – the skin is deep yellow, flecked with brown. As they ripen they give off ethylene gas, which can help other fruit – even green tomatoes – ripen as well. An avocado put in a lidded box with a banana should ripen overnight.

The banana's name betrays its history. It comes from a West African word, *banema*, originating from Guinea – from where the Portuguese took the fruit to the Canaries in 1402. From there banana roots arrived in America in 1516, courtesy of a Spanish missionary destined to become the Bishop of Panama.

Incidentally...

'Yes we have no bananas' became a popular wartime song in the food shortage days of the 1940s, though it had been written by Frank Silver and Irving Cohn long before, in 1923.

SERVE WHITE WINE WITH FISH, RED WITH MEAT

A helpful guide, not an unbreakable golden rule. The secret of success in matching wine with food is to think of the wine as another ingredient.

Following this logic, it makes perfect sense to enjoy an acid wine such as a Sauvignon, Riesling or Muscadet with fish in the same way that you would squeeze lemon over it. Similarly, a rich, full-bodied wine such as a Shiraz or Merlot is an excellent accompaniment to beef or game, while the acidity of a Cabernet Sauvignon makes it a perfect foil for rich roast pork.

In former times, wine was routinely bought by the cask and bottled at home. The butler was responsible for this task, and for laying down the wine.

If red is your preferred colour but fish your food, it is best to avoid wines high in tannins such as vintage Burgundies. But there are many good, light acidic reds to choose from, including young Riojas, Chiantis and Valpolicellas. For a white that will complement a meat dish, body is required, and you will get it from wines such as Pinot Gris, Chardonnay and Semillon.

Incidentally...

Some 800 years ago the School of Salerno in Italy defined the qualities of the perfect wine as five Fs: Fortia, formosa, et fragrantia, frigida, frisca, *which translates as: 'Strength, beauty, and fragrance, coolness, freshness.'*

AFTER MELON,
WINE IS A FELON

N ot only melon, but any sweet food, can ruin the taste of a wine. The rule for choosing wine to accompany sweet dishes is that it should be sweeter than the food.

This advice, and the mantras 'dry before sweet' and 'light before full' make melon a difficult ingredient to pair with wine at the start of a meal. But, if you match it with a savoury accompaniment such as Parma ham, a fruity German or New Zealand white wine would be a good choice.

Dessert wines have returned to favour, especially for home entertaining, and are the perfect match for sweet food. French Sauternes, not to be confused with the sugary Spanish or Californian 'Sauterne' gulped by the gallon by students in the 1960s (it was the only wine affordable and available), has a luscious intensity and is appropriate to serve with desserts such as strawberries and cream. Or choose an Australian Muscat or a Tokay, which will go well with even the sweetest chocolate mousse.

---

150 HORS D'OEUVRE RECIPES BY 'PIN' BAGLIONI OF THE EMBASSY CLUB, PUBLISHED IN 1934, INCLUDES A 'SPECIAL' FIRST COURSE IN WHICH CANTALOUPE MELON FLESH IS DICED AND SERVED (IN THE SCOOPED-OUT MELON HALVES) WITH A SAUCE MADE FROM A MIXTURE OF CURRY POWDER, GINGER, PORT, KIRSCH, WHIPPED CREAM, APRICOT PURÉE AND SUGAR!

In the grand houses and restaurants of the USA in the 1890s, champagne would often be served throughout a meal, 'with no other adjunct but bottled waters'. But, as the social advisor Constance Cary Harrison also remarked: 'How infinitely more welcome to the habitual diner out is a glass of good claret than indifferent champagne!'

NEVER BOIL COFFEE

Unless you want to risk a nasty tasting brew. Boiling coffee evaporates its aromatic oils and exaggerates its bitter tastes. It also breaks down some of the complex chemicals in the coffee beans into acids that make the drink taste sour, sharp and unpalatable.

Before the advent of coffee filtering – an innovation begun using a perforated china plate and attributed to JB de Belloy, an Archbishop of Paris who died in 1808 – boiling coffee was the accepted practice. Our modern palates would certainly not appreciate coffee made as recommended in the 1844 *Kitchen Directory and American Housewife*:

'Use a tablespoon ground to a pint of boiling water. Boil in a tin pot twenty to twenty-five minutes. If boiled longer it will not taste fresh and lively.

Incidentally...

Boiling coffee — or making it by any method that does not involve filtering — can be a health risk if you drink more than six cups of coffee a day. This is because boiling water releases from the beans the chemicals cafestol and kahweol, both of which are known to raise cholesterol levels. However, both are removed during filtering, and in instant coffee production.

Let stand four or five minutes to settle, pour off ground into a coffee pot or urn. Put fish skin or isinglass size of a ninepence in pot when put on to boil or else the white and shell of half an egg [to clear any cloudiness] to a couple of quarts of coffee.'

Today's filter coffee machines and percolators are designed to do just the opposite of this — to keep the water off the boil while encouraging the release of a wide variety of subtle aromas from the coffee. But whatever coffee making method you prefer, both the quality of beans and the roast are critical. The finest-tasting coffee comes from unblended arabica — not robusta — beans. A light or medium roast, which does not mar the beans' true taste, is preferable to a dark one.

THE CAFFEINE IN COFFEE NOT ONLY INCREASES ALERTNESS BUT HAS BEEN FOUND, IN STUDIES CONDUCTED AT THE UNIVERSITY OF SÃO PAULO AND REPORTED IN 2003, TO MAKE MEN'S SPERM SWIM MORE VIGOROUSLY.

ADD LEMON TO STRAWBERRY JAM TO MAKE IT SET

I f you're having real trouble getting jam to set, you also need to add pectin, the carbohydrate – which strawberries have too little of – that makes jams and jellies gel. Lemon juice helps the setting process by drawing out all the pectin that is available from the fruit.

The essential process of jam making is simple: boil the fruit with its own weight in sugar until, when a small amount is dabbed on to a cold plate, it cools to a firm consistency. While fruits like plums, currants and gooseberries contain plenty of natural pectin and jams made with them set with ease, strawberries and all but the most acid raspberries are notorious for their reluctance to set.

Incidentally...

The expression 'jam tomorrow', meaning a pleasant thing that remains a dream, comes from Lewis Carroll's Through the Looking Glass, *written in 1871. The White Queen offers Alice, in recompense for being her maid, twopence a week and jam every other day. Unfortunately for Alice, the deal is 'Jam to-morrow and jam yesterday – but never jam to-day.'*

Try boiling unpeeled lemon slices
and using the resulting liquid (which
contains pectin from the fruit pith)
or, to ensure success, use natural
pectin, which is available ready-
prepared in powder form or mixed
into special preserving sugar.

Jams are relative newcomers to the
kitchen cupboard, being first recorded
in the 1730s, some two hundred years
after solid marmalades and fruit
cheeses were originally made. Because
they needed so much sugar to ensure
a set and good keeping qualities, jams
remained a luxury. As Mrs Beeton
observed: 'The expense of preserving
them [fruits] with sugar is a serious
objection; for, except the sugar is used
in considerable quantities, the success is
very uncertain.'

HEALTH
AND BEAUTY

Though they may have followed the advice in ancient health manuals such as the Babylonian Code of Hammurabi, written in the 18th century BC, which included instructions for the use of herbs, ancient peoples also believed illness to be the vengeance of the gods and the work of evil spirits. Such spirits were thought to be deterred by a beautifully decorated body. Early cosmetics, such as the kohl applied around the eyes of Egyptian women, also helped to protect them from the sun and keep diseases at bay.

As medical knowledge advanced, people found it hard to shake off their belief in the old wives' tales. By the 19th century there was a huge trade in patent medicines, with secret formulae promising cures for everything from coughs to constipation and corns. Also widely advertised were beauty products for hair and skin and hinged appliances to replace missing limbs.

While they may not have been correct in every regard – like recommending butter for burns – it is remarkable how many of the old cures have been discovered by modern medical science to have a sound basis, whether it is the benefits of walking or laughter, that it is wise to stay out of the sun, or that fish is good for the brain.

WHITE FLECKS ON THE NAILS MEAN YOU'RE SHORT OF CALCIUM

They are more likely to be a sign that your diet is lacking zinc or possibly vitamin A, not calcium. For although calcium is needed for building strong bones and teeth, the nails are made of the fibrous protein keratin, which does not include calcium as one of its major components.

The link between calcium and white nail spots probably comes from the colour association — white spots, white mineral. In superstition they are associated with receiving gifts and predicting events, as in Ben Jonson's play *The Alchemist* of 1612: 'H'is a fortunate fellow, that I am sure on... And, in right way to'ward riches... I knew't, by certaine spots... on the nayle of his Mercurial [little] finger.'

Incidentally...

The nails can also betray serious disease. White streaks that run down the whole length of the nail can be a sign of heart disease and hollow, spoon-shaped nails can accompany severe iron deficiency. Pitted nails are typical of psoriasis.

To get more zinc, the easy way is to take a supplement of 30mg daily, plus 2mg of copper, which helps the zinc to be absorbed into the body more easily. Or it could be a good excuse to eat more oysters, which are rich in zinc, as are beef, the dark meat of poultry, liver, eggs and almonds. For men, as well as boosting nail health, zinc will help pep up the sperm count.

IT TAKES ABOUT SIX MONTHS FOR FINGERNAILS TO GROW FROM BASE TO TIP. THE NAILS GROW FASTER ON YOUR DOMINANT HAND.

DON'T KEEP PLANTS IN THE SICKROOM

Especially, it was said, at night time, for they would rob the room of vital oxygen. It is true that in darkness plants reverse their daytime activity of absorbing carbon dioxide and releasing oxygen but it would take more than a couple of vases of flowers to seriously affect the quality of the air.

Modern nurses have far greater concerns than removing plants from hospital wards at night, but our grandparents made much of the sickroom, which was entirely understandable in an era before the advanced antibiotics and inoculations that now cure or prevent so many illnesses.

The air of the sickroom was also likely to be polluted – at least in winter – by the fumes from a coal fire. However it was recommended that, except for patients suffering from chest and kidney complaints, the windows were 'opened wide after the action of the bowels'.

To prevent disturbing patients with unnecessary noise, maids were taught to use a gloved hand for putting coals on the fire one by one, or to wrap lumps of fuel in newspaper.

IT WAS CONSIDERED ESSENTIAL FOR THE OLD-FASHIONED SICKROOM TO BE CLEANED AND DUSTED EVERY DAY, AND THE PATIENT WASHED ALL OVER. FOR INFECTIOUS ILLNESS, A SHEET SOAKED IN A STRONG SOLUTION OF CARBOLIC OR THE DISINFECTANT LYSOL, MADE FROM COAL TAR, WAS HUNG OVER THE BEDROOM DOOR AND KEPT PERMANENTLY DAMP.

FRESHEN GARLIC BREATH BY CHEWING PARSLEY

The cook's favourite garnish is also one of the herbalist's traditional remedies for bad breath. Parsley stalks, rather than the leaves, will have the best effect, because they contain more of the plant's volatile oils.

Garlic is so potent on the breath because it is packed full of pungent sulphur-containing oils. These are carried in the blood to the lungs, released and breathed out through the mouth. In addition, smelly substances including hydrogen sulphide – the gas with the smell of bad eggs – are made from food remains by bacteria that live between the papillae, the tiny lobes in the tongue.

Brushing or scraping your tongue when you brush your teeth are ways of keeping these bacteria at bay.

Like other natural breath fresheners such as aniseed and peppermint, parsley will only mask offensive odours from foods like garlic and onions, or from drinking too much wine or beer, and will not cure the underlying effects of halitosis. If bad breath persists in the absence of garlic and its sulphurous relatives, it may be your teeth or gums that are the problem, or a persistent digestive ailment – for which parsley itself is a long-used herbal remedy.

Incidentally…

Chewing garlic was said to stop competitors getting ahead in races – as well as warding off vampires. Today, allicin, the chemical that gives fresh garlic its smell, is being used in hospitals to help fight 'superbugs' resistant to antibiotics.

NOT SURE WHETHER YOUR BREATH IS OFFENSIVE? AN OLD-FASHIONED TEST IS TO LICK THE BACK OF YOUR HAND, LET IT DRY FOR A FEW SECONDS, THEN SNIFF IT. IF IT SMELLS BAD, SO DOES YOUR BREATH.

ROSEHIP SYRUP
KEEPS COLDS AT BAY

This may be effective if you believe that mega doses of vitamin C are the best way to control the cold virus. Weight for weight, rosehips gathered from the dog rose (*Rosa canina*) actually contain over 20 per cent more vitamin C than oranges.

The idea of averting colds with doses of up to 10g a day of vitamin C was first advocated by the American Nobel laureate Linus Pauling in 1970. Counter to this, the latest research suggests that vitamin C reduces the duration of the symptoms rather than

Incidentally...

Rather than high-sugar syrup, rosehip tea is a good way of getting the health-giving vitamins of the hips. It can be made by infusing ½oz (15g) each of dried rosehips and chamomile flowers in 9fl oz (250ml) of boiling water, then sweetening the liquid with a little honey.

actually stopping a cold from occurring in the first instance. The other bad news is that there is virtually nothing that can stop the cold virus. But it's worth avoiding anyone who has just caught a cold, as the first three days of the illness are when a person is at their most infectious.

Even if it doesn't stop a cold, the vitamin C in rosehip syrup has lots of other health advantages. It fights the damage caused by 'free radicals' – unstable oxygen molecules – especially inside body cells, and in doing so helps to protect against cancer and heart disease.

ALWAYS CUT TOENAILS STRAIGHT ACROSS

Still the best way of preventing ingrowing toenails, the correct trimming of the nails is most easily done after a bath when they are soft.

When you cut into the sides of a big toenail, the 'nail folds' (the skin around the nail) can become swollen, and often painful and infected. Wearing shoes that are too tight can have the same effect – that is, to make the edge of the nail dig into the puffed-up skin. Despite the pain, it was known for schoolboys in the 1950s to inflict the problem on themselves to avoid compulsory games and cross-country runs.

At the first sign of an ingrowing toenail, the old-fashioned, painful treatment was to soak the toe in hot water for 10 minutes then raise the corner of the nail and press a piece of cotton wool under it. Today, antibiotics will most likely be prescribed to treat any infection, but scrupulous attention to hygiene is vital. In severe cases, the ingrowing nail will need to be professionally trimmed and surgery may be necessary to remove part of the nail base, from which it grows, narrowing the shape of the whole nail to avoid the problem recurring.

Nail cutting days

For the superstitious, the day of the week on which you cut your nails is crucial, as in this old rhyme:

Cut them on Monday,
  you cut them for health,

Cut them on Tuesday,
  you cut them for wealth,

Cut them on Wednesday,
  you cut them for news,

Cut them on Thursday,
  a new pair of shoes,

Cut them on Friday,
  you cut them for sorrow,

Cut them on Saturday,
  you see your true love tomorrow,

Cut them on Sunday,
  your safety seek,

The Devil will have you
  the rest of the week.

CUTTING THE HAIR MAKES IT STRONGER

Since the part of the hair that is cut is dead, this is unlikely, though even a trim will remove unsightly split ends and perk up your looks. It's just that your hair feels better and stronger when it's been scissored.

That hair is a source of strength goes back to the Biblical tale of Samson, whose mighty power was sapped when Delilah sneakily cut off his locks. The ancient Greeks believed that until a lock of hair was removed and devoted to the goddess Persephone the soul would not be released from a dying body.

Like the nails, the 100,000 or more hairs on our heads are made of the tough substance keratin. Only the base of the hair, the root, is alive, and from here the hair grows about an inch (25mm) every two to three months. The life of any individual hair is about two years for most people, though in the days when all girls grew their hair it was a great achievement to have hair so long that you could sit on it. That the hair was considered a girl's crowning glory made the ignominy of having the head shaved as a result of nit infestation even more shaming.

Incidentally...

Age-old natural treatments for stronger, better-looking hair include lemon juice to remove excess oil, castor oil applied an hour or two before shampooing to seal split ends, and the spice fenugreek taken daily as a herbal tea. This, we now know, contains an enzyme called triogonelline, which increases the blood supply to the scalp and allows more nutrients and oxygen to get to the follicles.

FISH IS GOOD FOR THE BRAIN

It is, and just as good for your heart – especially oily fish like salmon, mackerel and herring. Eating fish won't make you a genius, but will help to keep your whole nervous system in good shape.

What oily fish does best for the brain is to protect it from strokes – interruptions to the blood supply, often caused by blood clots, which kill brain cells and leave victims with anything from a slight paralysis on one side of the

Incidentally...

Eat the Japanese delicacy fugu – raw blowfish – and you could be taking your life in your hands. The skin, intestines, liver and roe contain a lethal toxin. Only specially trained fugu chefs may prepare it, but some Japanese are still fatally poisoned each year.

body to total loss of both memory and speech. The most effective substances in fish are omega-3 fatty acids, which help to keep the arteries clear. They may also help lift depression and even reduce the risk of dementia.

All fish benefit the nervous system by supplying good quantities of vitamin B12, and the oily varieties also provide vitamin A (vital for good eyesight) and D (for strong bones). And everyone can get at least a third of the protein they need each day by eating just 3½oz (100g) of any fish.

A swallowed fishbone can scratch the throat, making it feel as though it is stuck. If a bone is truly stuck, eating poorly chewed bread is a good way of dislodging it. Sipping neat lemon juice may help dissolve a small bone, but one that can't be shifted needs medical attention.

LATEST RESEARCH SUGGESTS THAT THE FATTY ACIDS IN FISH MAY HELP RECOVERY FROM CHRONIC FATIGUE SYNDROME BY EFFECTING 'REPAIRS' IN THE BRAIN.

ADAM'S ALE
IS THE BEST BREW

That is water, the world's first drink, named from the first man, and the fluid vital to life. Its importance is shown in its symbolic use in Christian baptism, named from the Greek *baptizein*, meaning 'to dip in water'.

The adult body, which itself is about 60 per cent water, needs water for keeping all its parts well lubricated and for essential tasks such as digestion. And since water is continuously expelled as we breathe, as well as in the other processes of living, it needs to be constantly replaced.

Incidentally…

In Christian baptism candidates may immerse themselves fully or have the sign of the cross made on their foreheads with holy water. The rite of baptism expresses both the pardoning of sins and the gift of eternal life.

Luckily, most food is also water-rich (we get about a quarter of all the water we need from what we eat, and most of all from fruit and vegetables), but the experts reckon that we should all drink around 4½ pints (2 litres) of water a day just to keep the system topped up, and more if we exercise vigorously and lose water in sweat. Dehydration makes you feel headachy, sluggish and lethargic and can be a precipitating factor in conditions such as kidney stones and urinary infections.

The health-giving properties of the water at spa towns has long been appreciated. Bath, which was developed by the Romans, became a medieval destination for pilgrims in search of healing cures. In Europe, places such as Baden-Baden in Germany and Spa in Belgium became fashionable places to 'take the waters' from the 16th century.

As for today's water, hard high-mineral tap water is healthier than soft. And all tap water, as long as it is guaranteed free from bacterial contamination, is as good for you (and your pocket) as bottled water, which can be high in sodium.

THE FIRST WATER DRAWN FROM A WELL ON NEW YEAR'S DAY WAS THOUGHT, IN COUNTRY DISTRICTS, TO ENDOW GOOD FORTUNE IF SPRINKLED ON PASSERS-BY. IF DRUNK IT WAS ALSO BELIEVED TO BRING BEAUTY AND WEALTH.

PALE IS BEAUTIFUL

Especially if you want to avoid sunburn and, ultimately, skin cancer. Until the 1920s, when the suntan first became fashionable, a 'lady' would do everything possible to avoid having a reddened or tanned skin like that of a farmworker.

When exposed to the sun the skin reacts by producing extra amounts of the dark, protective substance melanin, but fair skins can easily get burnt well before this happens. Cells are probably triggered to become cancerous by the sun's UVA and UVB rays, especially if the skin is overexposed to them during childhood.

Avoiding the sun between 11am and 3pm, covering up and using a sunscreen with a high protection factor (30 plus, or a total block in the case of fair skin) are the proven ways to cut the risk. Do not forget vulnerable spots such as the lips and the backs of the knees and, if you do burn, apply calamine lotion or aloe vera to help cool the skin and speed healing.

When bicycling became the vogue in the late 19th century *Cycling Hints for Ladies* suggested: 'A veil [worn over a hat]… as a protection against flies, and to conceal a flushed face,' and 'To avoid sunburn, if the skin is delicate, a lady should, before starting, rub glycerine in. If the skin is already affected by the sun, either milk or lemon juice, glycerine or cucumber, or sulpholine lotion is very useful.'

Incidentally…

Get a hat. Headwear with a brim 4in (10cm) wide can cut your risk of skin cancer by up to 40 per cent.

COLD HANDS, WARM HEART

A saying true for the body, if not the soul. When we get cold the circulation in our extremities closes down to protect the inner organs – the heart included – which is why it is possible to survive severe frostbite in both hands and feet.

Like other warm-blooded animals, the bodies of humans are tuned to maintain a constant temperature – in our case 98.6°F (37°C). As soon as our internal sensors register that we are getting cold, our self-protective mechanisms go into action. First we get goosebumps as our hair stands on end in an attempt to improve body insulation. Then we shiver, generating warmth through muscle movement. Simultaneously, blood is diverted to the body's core, shielding key organs from potentially fatal blood clots and strokes.

Incidentally...

In the condition known as Raynaud's syndrome the blood vessels in the extremities – not only the hands but also the feet, ears and nose – may go into spasm when subjected to cold, cutting off the circulation. The affected parts go white and numb, and when the spasm eases become red and painful. The problem affects about one person in ten and is much more common in women than men.

Apart from wearing gloves, exercise to get the circulation going is a good way of keeping the hands warm. Or it can be pepped up with ginger, a spice long renowned for dilating the blood vessels and stimulating the circulation: it tastes especially good mixed with lemon, honey and hot water.

Servants such as scullery maids, with their hands constantly in water, suffered greatly from raw, chapped hands. But in the early 20th century they were advised that: 'Vigorous scrubbing with a soft nailbrush when washing stimulates the circulation... For chapped hands, clarified mutton fat, perfumed to liking, is a simple but efficacious remedy.'

IF COLD HANDS MEAN A WARM HEART, A MOIST HAND IS SAID TO BETRAY AN AMOROUS NATURE.

HIGH HEELS GIVE YOU BACKACHE

They can, because they shift your centre of gravity and put extra strain on the spine. But for many women there is no confidence booster to beat the stiletto.

High heels put the spine out of kilter by transferring the weight forwards from the heels (which bear, together with the hips and backbone, most of the body's weight) to the toes. Though it helps to have an ankle support to prevent the toes from 'clawing' as they try to keep the shoe on the foot, high heels affect some people more adversely than others. Trouble is most likely if the extra height adds an exaggerated curve to your lower spine, making you hollow-backed.

If worn every day of the week, high heels can exacerbate bunions as well as backache, but sometimes only a high heel will do. Late Victorian women were advised that when 'the heel is placed exactly in the right spot… and the slipper fits snugly and comfortably… it is no more injurious to wear under these conditions than any other well fitting shoe, and gives a certain elasticity to the carriage of the graceful woman that a flat shoe never does.'

The stiletto, fashion essential of the 1960s, harked back to the French court of the 17th and 18th centuries, when heels were first worn by men (to add to their height) and then by both sexes. Stilettos are named from the tapered instrument used to pierce eyelets in leather. (The stiletto dagger has a short, thick blade.)

If you warm cold feet too quickly you'll get chilblains

What causes chilblains is getting your feet very cold, but you only feel them some time afterwards, when the pain and almost unbearable itching begin. In the days when houses were so cold that ice formed overnight on the inside of the windows, chilblains were a common complaint.

When the blood vessels just under the skin get cold they go into spasm, cutting down the blood supply and damaging the cells. This results in inflammation – which is exacerbated by fast warming – and purple-red chilblains, known medically as erythema pernio. If very severe, cracks and blisters can appear, which, if not professionally treated, can lead to ulcers or even gangrene.

Keeping warm and well wrapped, and exercising vigorously in cold weather so that blood circulates freely through all the extremities, is the best way of preventing chilblains. Ginger, mustard and capsicum, which warm the skin and help to improve the circulation, are among the tried and tested herbal treatments.

Today, effective over-the-counter remedies can be bought for itching chilblains, but past sufferers would mix their own concoctions. One 19th-century recipe consisted of 'One raw egg well beaten, half a pint of vinegar, one ounce of spirits of turpentine, a quarter of an ounce of spirits of wine, a quarter of an ounce of camphor.' Broken chilblains could have been treated for a day or two with a bread and water poultice, then with calamine or zinc oxide.

Incidentally...

An old Romany remedy for chilblains is to bathe them for 20 minutes in the (unsalted) water in which parsnips have been boiled, with a tablespoon of powdered alum added. It is recommended that the liquid should not be rinsed off but allowed to dry on the skin.

FEED A COLD, STARVE A FEVER

This is not just an old wives' tale but advice that really works. For colds, chicken soup passes the scientists' health test too.

Researchers at the Academic Medical Centre in Amsterdam have discovered that food (given as a 1,200-calorie liquid meal) boosted blood levels of gamma interferon, a substance we produce to fight viruses such as those that cause colds and flu. But they also found that after fasting for 12 hours there is a rise in blood levels of the protein interleucin-4, a substance made by the antibodies to combat severe infections such as typhoid, which cause high fever.

So is chicken soup the perfect food for a cold? A team working at Nebraska Medical Center found that for people with colds chicken soup – whether home

Incidentally...

In the 17th century Jesuit missionaries in South America discovered that the bark of the chinchona tree could lower the fever of malaria. Its active component – quinine – destroys malarial parasites in blood, but is highly toxic, even in moderate doses.

made or canned – reduced inflammation and helped stopped noses running by
easing the production of excess mucus. Plain vegetable soup with no chicken
did not work as well. News on the exact ingredients in chicken that help a cold
are not yet forthcoming.

A fever – the body's way of coping with a severe infection – is always more
serious than a cold, especially in children. In the days before vaccinations and
antibiotics the hope was always that a patient would 'come through' a fever
alive, whatever their age.

PUT VINEGAR ON A WASP STING

O r rub it with a cut onion, great-
grandmother would have said.
Unlike a bee, which leaves
its sting in the skin (it needs to be
carefully removed with tweezers),
the wasp usually injects its poison
then flies off to sting again.

The best wasp sting remedies – lemon
juice is another – neutralize the
alkalinity of the sting. An ice pack will
help calm any swelling. It was once
thought that the toxin could travel to
and poison the heart. In fact what can
be fatal following both wasp and bee

Wasps are nature's paper makers: they chew leaves and wood fibres, mixing them with saliva to make a pulp, which they use for nest building. Some South American wasps add soil to the pulp to make nest walls that are as solid as stone.

stings is anaphylaxis, an extreme allergic reaction in which the air passages swell up and breathing is fatally impaired.

In late summer, wasps in orchards were traditionally trapped in jars filled with beer or sugared water hung in the trees. Enticed to drink, the insects would drown.

In the past sulphur was used to fumigate wasps' nests, but a more humane solution is to leave it until the end of the season, when the colony will disappear anyway, then block off the hole or crevice in which it formed.

ACCORDING TO PLINY'S *NATURAL HISTORY* OF AD 77, THE FIRST WASP OF THE YEAR, TIED UNDER A PATIENT'S CHIN, WOULD CURE A FEVER.

COUGHS AND SNEEZES SPREAD DISEASES

'…Trap the germs in your handkerchief.' So ran the slogan on the British 1942 wartime poster, when food and fuel were scarce and health at a premium. And beware of touching anything – microbes can easily spread on everything, from fingers to doorknobs and pieces of paper.

The germs – bacteria and viruses – that cause disease are forced from the body at high speed in coughs and sneezes, which makes these a simple and effective way for germs to spread from person to person. But the diseases that make us sneeze and splutter – especially colds and flu – are also spread by touch, so as well as avoiding the newly infectious, deter infection by washing your hands, especially if you've been handed anything by someone with a cold, and avoid touching your mouth or nose until you have done so.

The good handkerchief was still much prized when *The House and Home Practical Book* of 1896 declared: 'When it comes to certain accessories of the toilet, notably handkerchiefs, every American woman has cause to regret that she was not born in Paris. The French handkerchiefs are so superior in texture, in ornamentation and so maddeningly cheap in comparison.' However, it continued, 'so called fancy handkerchiefs, made of chiffon are... not to be recommended... its adoption as an ornament is not to be sanctioned...'

Incidentally...

Coughing is the tell-tale symptom of consumption – pulmonary tuberculosis – which in the 1890s accounted for three in every 20 deaths of New Yorkers and is still a major cause of death worldwide, mainly in Southeast Asia and Africa. In the course of the disease, blood is commonly coughed up.

IF YOU COUGH A LOT, CHECK YOUR EARS: A SEVERE BUILD-UP OF EAR WAX CAN PRESS ON THE NERVE THAT TRIGGERS THE COUGH REFLEX.

KEEP YOUR TEETH: BRUSH THEM WITH SALT

Brushing with salt helps to keep infections at bay. Just brushing is important, as is flossing between your teeth – a recommendation with origins centuries old.

The secret of salt is that it spells death to the bacteria that infect both teeth and gums; ultimately it can be gum disease that, when it spreads into the jaw bones, makes people lose their teeth. Yet another reason for keeping gums healthy is that there is a link between gum infection and both strokes and heart disease.

Brushing at a 45° angle, and getting the bristles just under the gum line, are what dentists recommend for good oral hygiene to minimize the build-up of plaque in which bacteria thrive. A professional scaling every three to six months to get rid of the plaque that has hardened into tartar is also recommended.

Incidentally...

The Chinese made the first toothbrushes from bristle in the 17th century. They were 're-invented' in the West 150 years later, when the Englishman William Addis made brushes with ox bone handles and pig bristles. Before brushes, wooden 'chewing sticks' were favoured.

Early tooth cleaners were harsh, abrasive powders; softer chalk was not added until the 1850s. Even then, housewives made their own 'dentifrices', which could include powdered soap, clove oil and rose water. One recipe for 'American Tooth Powder' called for coral, cuttlefish bone, dragon's blood [a tree resin], burnt alum, red sanders [sandalwood], orris root, cloves, cinnamon, vanilla, rosewood and rose-pink [a pink pigment], all finely powdered and mixed.

GROOVES IN TEETH EXCAVATED FROM PREHISTORIC SITES SUGGEST THAT EARLY HUMANS CLEANED THEIR TEETH WITH BOTH TOOTHPICKS AND FLOSS. MODERN FLOSS, ORIGINALLY MADE OF SILK, WAS 'INVENTED' BY THE NEW ORLEANS DENTIST LEVI SPEAR PARMLY, WHO FIRST PROMOTED ITS USE IN 1815.

SLEEPING ON YOUR BACK MAKES YOU SNORE

Yes it does, but there are other reasons, too, such as having a cold that blocks up your nose. Night-time nuisance aside, one type of snoring can lead to a life-threatening lack of oxygen.

'There ain't no way,' said Mark Twain in *Tom Sawyer Abroad* (1894), 'to find out why a snorer can't hear himself snore.' This is a sentiment shared by many a wife whose husband is oblivious to night-time noise reaching 80 decibels (the maximum set by Vancouver traffic bylaws) or more: this isn't a sexist

observation since serious male snorers far outnumber female ones.

Snoring is the sound of the soft tissues of the throat vibrating. It happens when air pushed out from the lungs rushes through constricted passages – such as when you lie on your back and your tongue lolls towards your throat, partially blocking it. Other factors come into play, too. If you're overweight fatty tissue can narrow your airways, and the relaxing effect of alcohol makes them loose and vibratory.

Snoring becomes dangerous when the amount of oxygen getting to the lungs is seriously impaired. This is the condition called sleep apnoea, which needs medical attention and is typified by loud, frequent and irregular snoring, with interruptions that sound as if the snorer has stopped breathing.

IF YOU WANT TO STOP SNORING, FORCE YOURSELF TO SLEEP ON YOUR SIDE: MAKE A POCKET IN THE BACK OF YOUR PYJAMAS OR NIGHTDRESS AND INSERT A TENNIS BALL OR A LARGE MARBLE TO DETER YOU FROM ROLLING ON TO YOUR BACK.

CURE A HANGOVER WITH THE 'HAIR OF THE DOG THAT BIT YOU'

I n other words another drink. This is effective, but only because it puts recovery on hold. Popular cures for the thumping head and sandpaper mouth have been invented in every age.

There are good reasons why alcohol produces hangovers. It causes dehydration; it reduces blood sugar levels; when it is being processed by the liver it produces toxic by-products; and it contains chemicals, including methanol, that contaminate the system. Alcohol in drinks comes in two sorts, ethanol and methanol, which the liver tackles in that order. When it starts on the methanol it begins to produce its dire effects, releasing formic acid into the system. Having another drink puts the liver back into ethanol-processing mode, delaying the methanol effect.

Incidentally...

The expression 'hair of the dog' comes from the medieval belief that a cure for a dog bite could be effected by burning some of the hair from the dog's tail and inserting it in the wound.

Anything that raises blood sugar levels and restores water to the system will help a hangover. This could be anything from a fatty bacon sandwich downed with large quantities of water or tea to paracetemol (acetaminophen) swallowed with a mashed banana and a pint of sweetened orange juice.

LINE YOUR STOMACH: ALCOHOL IS ABSORBED MORE SLOWLY IF YOU EAT BEFORE YOU DRINK, ESPECIALLY FATTY OR HIGH-CARBOHYDRATE FOODS.

Some hangover remedies through the ages

Ancient Greeks – Fried cabbage; the warm entrails of a freshly slaughtered sheep.

Ancient Romans – Fried canaries.

16th century – Raw eels and almonds, ground to a paste, eaten with bread.

17th century – Bleeding by leeches.

18th century – A sugar cube soaked with clove oil, parsley and honey.

1880s – John Stith Pemberton's tonic (destined to become Coca-Cola), which contained cocaine, caffeine and alcohol dissolved in caramel syrup and diluted in carbonated water.

20th century – The fry-up.

21st century – RU-21, a mixture of vitamin C, carbohydrates and amino acids developed by the KGB to keep spies up to the mark.

CARE BRINGS GREY HAIR

A saying that originates from the way in which the hair can apparently turn grey overnight, but whether it begins when you're 30 or 60, grey hair is usually an inevitable family inheritance.

The prisoner in Byron's poem 'The Prisoner of Chillon' (1816) begins his story by asserting:

> *My hair is grey,*
> *   but not with years,*
> *Nor grew it white*
> *In a single night,*
> *As men's have grown*
> *   from sudden fears.*

In fact, hair goes grey when pigment-producing cells in the hair follicles stop making melanin, the substance that gives hair its colour. By the time you see they are grey the hairs are already dead, so there's no point in pulling them out in the hope of something better! A severe shock or illness can make hair fall out, giving the impression that the hair has suddenly gone grey and, when it grows back, it can be paler.

Plants, particularly the mature leaves of henna, *Lawsonia inermia*, have been used for at least 5,000 years to colour the hair – and also for ceremonial decoration of the hands and nails. Some boiling water poured over a couple of handfuls of dried cornflowers (*Centaurea cyanus*), infused for a few hours and strained, makes a traditional herbal rinse that tints grey hair a delicate blue.

Incidentally…

In men, hair and beard do not always turn grey simultaneously.
'Greybeard' is a complimentary term for a wise old man – and also
a word for a Flemish stoneware liquor pot named (in ridicule) for
Cardinal Bellarmine, who lived from 1542 to 1621.

AN APPLE A DAY KEEPS THE DOCTOR AWAY

A 19th-century saying that may have arisen because no other fruit is cultivated and eaten in more countries of the world. Like other fruit, apples do you good because, among other things, they are rich in vitamins and fibre.

Apples promote a healthy circulation and immune system because they contain vitamin C and (in their skins) flavonoids, both anti-oxidants that also help keep arteries clear of clogging cholesterol. Their soluble fibre helps cure constipation and their plant sugar fructose, metabolized more slowly than glucose, provides sustained energy. To make a 'cooling drink for sick persons', *Enquire Within* in the 1890s recommended: 'a tart apple well baked and mashed, on which pour a pint of boiling water. Beat up, cool and strain. Add sugar if desired.'

But an apple a day also 'keeps the dentist in pay'. For although eating a crunchy apple scrapes plaque-forming bacteria off the teeth, acids in the fruit pulp soften tooth enamel while the sugars provide ready sustenance for the microbes of decay (see p 170).

UPON REACHING THE NEW WORLD, THE PILGRIM FATHERS PLANTED APPLES AS ONE OF THEIR FIRST CROPS. JOHNNY APPLESEED WAS THE NICKNAME FOR JOHN CHAPMAN, BORN IN LEOMINSTER, MASSACHUSETTS, ON 26 SEPTEMBER 1774. FROM ABOUT 1800, HE COLLECTED SEEDS AND PLANTED THEM ACROSS THE CONTINENT, CREATING NURSERIES FROM THE EAST COAST TO OHIO AND INDIANA.

FATS MAKE YOU FAT

Because fats are more packed with calories than other foods, eating them to excess can help pile on the pounds. But when food was scarce, plumpness was a sign of affluence and, in women like those depicted by the Flemish painter Sir Peter Paul Rubens in *The Three Graces* (1639), a mark of sensuality.

We enjoy eating fats because they not only give food a good flavour but impart a smooth texture that makes it slip down easily – the crucial difference between dry bread and bread and butter, or old-fashioned bread and dripping (the solidified fat from a roast joint). And no matter whether they are 'good' unsaturated fats, like olive oil, or 'bad' saturated fats from animal products (the ones linked to heart disease), all pure fats supply us with about 250 kilo-calories per ounce (9 calories per gram). By comparison, even pure carbohydrate such as sugar contains only about 111 calories per ounce (4 calories per gram).

Incidentally...

Weight Watchers was founded in 1961 by Jean Nidetch, an overweight New York City housewife who initially formed a support group with her friends for mutual advice and encouragement.

When it comes to weight the simple truth is that if you take in more calories than you burn then your body stores the excess as fat. That obesity is a problem today is exemplified by the fact that while in 1900 Americans obtained on average 30 per cent of their daily calories from fat, by 2000 it was at least 40 per cent — between six and eight times as much as the body needs for essential jobs such as cell maintenance and repair.

You should breakfast like a king... and dine like a pauper

The first meal of the day, the end of the night's 'fast' is the chance to replenish energy supplies. And there is mounting evidence that people who eat a good breakfast have less trouble controlling their weight than those who don't.

In studies of eating behaviour, researchers discovered that slimmers who eat breakfast consume fewer calories for the rest of the day than those who do not and, as a bonus, find it easier to stick to a calorie-controlled diet. Other trials confirm that high-fibre foods eaten early in the day are effective at taming hunger and that giving children cereal for breakfast seems to be a good way of preventing them from gaining excess weight.

So does eating late at night make you fat? The idea that going to sleep soon after eating allows the body insufficient time to burn off calories is now thought to be erroneous. What matters is the total calories eaten during the day — and the number burnt off by exercise.

On the farm, milk and eggs, direct from dairy and henhouse, were the natural, readily available breakfast choices. Over the years other foods became breakfast favourites; in the grand 19th-century home bacon, kidneys (often devilled), kippers, kedgeree, sausages, tomatoes and mushrooms would be on offer for guests, served in the dining room or a separate breakfast room.

Incidentally...

Compared with porridge (see p 121), ready-to-eat breakfast cereals are newcomers to the breakfast table. Brothers Will and John Harvey Kellogg marketed their first packets of cornflakes in 1898, backed up by a powerful health message.

KEDGEREE – A CURRIED DISH OF SMOKED FISH, RICE AND HARD BOILED EGGS – WAS A POPULAR IMPORT TO BRITAIN IN THE DAYS OF THE RAJ. THE ORIGINAL BREAKFAST DISH, *KHICHRI*, MADE FROM MUNG BEANS AND RICE, HAS BEEN MADE AND ENJOYED FOR CENTURIES.

Stress gives you ulcers

For most people with ulcers in the stomach or duodenum – and in the mouth – the primary cause is infection. But stress, because it can lower your immunity, doesn't help.

In the intestine, it is the bacterium *Helicobacter (H.) pylori* that is the culprit in forming ulcers. It is estimated that half the population harbour it – probably from childhood – though only a fifth of these actually develop ulcers. In a peptic ulcer, which can affect the oesophagus, stomach or duodenum, the lining of the intestine is attacked and eroded by acid juices.

Antibiotics, combined with drugs to inhibit acid production – or to neutralize it, once secreted – are the conventional treatments for peptic ulcers, but there are many traditional remedies. These include liquorice root, which increases the secretion of the protective, sticky substance mucin in the gut, and 'miraculous' mastic gum, which has been used to treat digestive complaints for over 3,000 years and is produced from the tree *Pistachia lentiscus*, which grows exclusively on the Greek island of Chios. The bonus of mastic gum is that it also deals a knockout blow to the *Herpes simplex* viruses that cause mouth ulcers.

ALTHOUGH THE ULCER-PRONE ARE ADVISED TO AVOID IRRITANTS SUCH AS TOBACCO SMOKE, ALCOHOL AND SPICES, THEY NO LONGER FACE THE OLD TREATMENTS OF BED REST, BLAND FOOD AND 'FREE ADMINISTRATION OF BISMUTH AND ALKALIS'.

DRINKING SEA WATER TURNS YOU MAD

It also, ironically, kills you from thirst because it is three times too salty for the kidneys to cope with. Drinking it therefore causes dehydration, which brings on delirium because the workings of the brain cells are severely disrupted.

Sea water is salty because it contains large quantities of sodium chloride, as well as salts of other minerals such as potassium. And although we all need some sodium to keep our cells functioning properly, and to replace what we lose in sweat, too much of it draws essential water out of the cells and eventually kills them.

Should you ever find yourself adrift at sea, the best advice is to resist drinking any fresh water you have for 24 hours and to ration supplies to about 1¾ pints (1 litre) a day per person. Don't even use sea water to dampen your lips. Try to relieve thirst by sucking a button or pebble, which will stimulate the salivary glands.

Incidentally...

In 1820, the whaling ship Essex left Nantucket, Massachusetts, bound for South America. In the middle of the Pacific Ocean she was rammed by a sperm whale and capsized. As their supplies of food and drink ran out, the crew began drinking sea water, which sent them mad and eventually started to kill them. Those who survived did so by 'the custom of the sea' – eating their dead companions. The diary of the First Mate, Owen Chase, is believed to have influenced Herman Melville, who read it 30 years later while writing Moby Dick.

NANNY
KNOWS BEST

Long gone is the era when children were 'seen but not heard', but there is still much to be admired – and much that is still true – in old-fashioned childcare advice. But there are few modern parents who would, or could, insist on their offspring chewing each mouthful 20 times or always sleeping with the window open.

Before effective medicines and inoculations were available to treat and ward off diseases, and before the basics of a healthy diet were understood, childhood was hazardous. Survival would certainly have taken the upper hand over etiquette until the 15th century when *The Babees' Book* of manners, including advice on good behaviour, cleanliness and table manners, was published.

Until the early 20th century the children of the wealthy were raised by nannies and governesses but, following World War I, many mothers found themselves without home helps. Early childcare manuals such as Sir Frederick Truby King's *Feeding and Care of Baby* (1928) advocated regimes of timed feeds and strict discipline – a stark contrast with today's relaxed attitudes, fostered by books like Dr Benjamin Spock's *Baby and Child Care*, first published in 1946 when the 'baby boom' was in full swing.

SIT UP STRAIGHT

With 'stand up straight', this is one of the cardinal rules of good posture, because sitting and standing tall not only help to strengthen the back but also improve self-confidence.

Sitting and standing up straight are good for the back because they set the shoulders and spine in correct alignment with the hips – the joints that bear the bulk of the body's weight. They also help to tone up the abdominal muscles which, although they do not make contact with the backbone, assist the muscles that do so, and keep the internal organs well girdled.

Good posture was a must for the carefully reared child of the 19th century. 'Nothing,'

Incidentally...

The Alexander technique is based on the principle that improved posture benefits the entire body and helps cure problems such as persistent headaches. Devised by the Australian actor Frederick Matthias Alexander in the late 19th century, after he began to lose his voice on stage, it teaches people how to 'stand tall' as if their heads are attached to the ceiling by a piece of string.

says a guide to mothers of the 1890s, 'can be worse for a weak back than sitting forward in a heap.' Even until the 1960s, girls' schools encouraged perfect deportment with prizes for excellence and regular exercises such as walking while balancing a heavy book on the head. For today's children, books carried in a heavy rucksack are more likely to be a problem, especially if the bag is hung on one shoulder, which risks setting up back problems for later life.

THE SPINE IS MADE UP OF 24 BONES OR VERTEBRAE. BETWEEN THE VERTEBRAE ARE FIBROUS DISCS THAT ACT AS SHOCK ABSORBERS.

EAT YOUR CRUSTS – THEY'LL MAKE YOUR HAIR CURL

This is not true, but the fiction was understandable when crusts were hard, food too precious to be wasted and straight hair was considered plain and dull.

Even when bobs came into fashion in the 1920s, curls were still desirable, and only with Vidal Sassoon's geometric cuts of the 1960s did they finally go 'out'. Curling the hair could be a messy, often painful business. Throughout the ancient Near East, women coated their hair in wet clay, let it dry and combed out their tresses into

Whether your hair curls or not depends on heredity. Our genes determine the shape of the follicles below the scalp from which hairs originate, and if they make the hair grow unevenly it will be curly.

waves. The ringlets
of well-to-do Greek
women were created
using curling tongs,
a device 're-invented'
in the 1870s by the
Parisian hairdresser
Marcel Grateau to create
the popular 'Marcel wave'.

Rags and metal curlers were popular too,
often left in overnight or even all day under
a headscarf. The first permanent waves,
introduced in London in 1906, involved using
borax paste and brass curlers that weighed
over 24lb (12kg) and had to be left in the hair
for six hours. But the perm caught on, and
in the early days of commercial television, classic advertising slogans for home
perms (based on the cold perm of 1945) included 'Which twin has the Toni?'
and 'Friday night is Amami night'.

AT POLITE AFTERNOON TEA, WHICH BECAME THE HEIGHT OF
FASHION FROM THE MID-19TH CENTURY UNTIL AFTER WORLD
WAR II, CUCUMBER SANDWICHES WERE ALWAYS SERVED WITH
THE CRUSTS REMOVED.

Before the days of the steam-baked loaf and the ubiquitous sliced bread, introduced in the 1930s as Wonder Loaf, crusts could be really hard going, especially on bread that was more than a day old. Leftover crusts were baked in a low oven to make rusks for any teething babies in the family. On the plus side, chewing crusts is good for the gums and bread is a great food packed with energy and vitamins.

DON'T SCRATCH AN ITCH

There is nothing more irritating than an itch, but this adage is pure common sense because, in the end, scratching will only prolong the agony.

It is histamine that makes you want to scratch an itch. This is the chemical released into the skin when you are bitten by an insect or stung by a nettle or jellyfish, or when you have a disease like chickenpox. It is also produced when you develop an allergic reaction to something that touches your skin, like soap or the metal nickel, or to a certain food. What happens when you scratch is that even more histamine is produced, making you want to scratch even more.

Incidentally...

Long-used herbal preparations for soothing itchy skin include lavender ointment and an infusion of dried marigold flowers.

Over-the-counter antihistamines will help the symptoms, but it is well worth tracking down the cause of an allergy so as to avoid it in future. Granny's remedies for itching were calamine lotion, a dilute (1 in 40) solution of carbolic acid, or a warm soda bath before bed. For young children tempted to scratch the treatment was severe: '[They] should be prevented from scratching by sewing the sleeves of their nightdress to the body of the garment, or by loosely tying the hands to the waist.'

AN ITCHING PALM IS SAID TO REVEAL A PERSON READY TO RECEIVE BRIBES OR, ACCORDING TO SUPERSTITION, IS A SIGN THAT MONEY IS ON ITS WAY. AN ITCHING EAR, ON THE OTHER HAND, BETRAYS SOMEONE EAGER TO ENJOY SCANDAL OR GOSSIP.

BRUSH YOUR HAIR A HUNDRED TIMES AT NIGHT

A hundred is too many, but brushing certainly makes hair shine by stimulating the oil glands in the scalp, and distributing oil evenly along the length of the tresses. But overbrushing can damage both hair and scalp.

The other problem with brushes and combs is that they can pull out hairs or make the ends split or break off. Too much brushing may overstimulate the oil glands and make the hair too greasy, especially in the teenage years when the

Incidentally…

Brilliantine, containing almond or castor oil, or produced in solid form with a petroleum jelly base, was the traditional way of making the hair shine before the introduction of products such as Brylcreem in 1937.

production of sebum, the natural, protective hair oil, is being boosted by a surge of hormones.

It would have taken a great deal of brushing or combing before bedtime to untangle some of the complex women's hairstyles of the past, and even a girl's plaits if her hair was naturally curly. In the days when long hair was *de rigueur*, standard night-time advice lectured against the use of fine combs, which would 'tear out hair unnecessarily', and recommended that to protect it from strain on the roots during sleep 'hair should never be fastened up very tightly… the more loosely it is plaited the better'.

A lock of hair was a lovers' keepsake and a sign of fidelity. Locks of hair were often exchanged before men went off to war.

CHOOSE PINK FOR A GIRL, BLUE FOR A BOY

When it comes to good fortune in colours, girls get the raw deal. Because, in a family, boys were once more highly prized than girls, they became linked with the colour that is traditionally associated with good fortune.

Blue, the colour of the sky, has long been a lucky hue, and the *Book of Numbers*, written in the 5th century BC, advised the children of Israel to protect themselves by wearing garments fringed with 'a ribband of blue'. Wearing a blue ribbon or necklace was also thought to protect against illness – but so too was donning a red one. A red thread worn around the neck was supposed, from the 1st century AD onwards, to guard against problems as diverse as

Incidentally...

The all-in-one stretch 'Babygro' was devised by a father frustrated with dressing his child. It was patented in 1959.

lunacy and a witch's evil eye.

Swaddling bands were the usual clothing for babies until the 1700s. After this a layette including gowns and petticoats was gradually introduced. Only in the early 1900s did boys and girls come to be dressed differently, and it was the 1930s before the fashion for pink and blue really took hold.

A matter of luck

A bride invokes blue's lucky powers when she chooses 'something blue' to wear, along with something old, something new and something borrowed.

It is said that, for luck, newborn babies should be dressed by pulling the clothes over their feet, not their heads.

In Ireland, boy babies were often – until the 20th century – dressed as girls in an attempt to deceive the 'boy-seeking Devil'.

DON'T SWALLOW CHERRY STONES – THEY CAN GIVE YOU APPENDICITIS

Lack of fibre in the diet, not pips and stones, is thought to be the most likely cause of appendicitis. Fruit stones will, very rarely, lodge in the appendix, but are most likely to pass through the digestive system and be ejected from the body intact.

Appendicitis – infection, obstruction and inflammation of the 'redundant' 3½in (9cm) pouch in the large intestine – is most common in young people between the ages of eight and 25. Usually, there is no obvious reason for the problem, but it can be associated with constipation – the 'stones' that are sometimes detected during surgery are in fact small, hard faeces.

Incidentally...

The term appendicitis was first used in the USA by Dr Reginald Fitz in 1886. In Britain, the first appendectomy was performed on Samuel Smith at the London Hospital in 1888 by the Dorset surgeon Frederick Treves. But while Fitz believed in surgery immediately following diagnosis, Treves recommended waiting five days: the belief cost him the life of his own daughter, who died from a ruptured appendix.

The typical symptoms of appendicitis are a pain around the navel, which (though not always in children) moves downwards and to the right, and is worse after the release of pressure if the area is pressed. Acute appendicitis needs emergency surgery: if the problem organ ruptures it can lead to potentially fatal septicaemia (blood poisoning).

Some experts still believe in the 'grumbling' appendix – painful attacks that resolve themselves spontaneously – but others think that an appendix either 'roars' because it is inflamed or is healthy and silent.

The cherry stones on your plate were counted in the old rhyme 'Tinker, tailor, soldier, sailor, rich man, poor man, beggar man, thief', to predict whom you would marry.

DON'T SWIM UNTIL AT LEAST AN HOUR AFTER A MEAL

The logic here is that immediately after eating the legs may be more susceptible to cramp, increasing the risk of drowning. And although modern medicine takes a somewhat less prescriptive view, it remains wise to be cautious of heavy meals and remote beaches.

It is a fact that immediately after a meal, blood is diverted to the stomach and digestive system. As a result it is drawn away from the arms and legs, depriving their muscles of water, nutrients and the minerals they need to contract smoothly and painlessly. Equally, there is a known link between regular, persistent cramp – strong localized muscle contractions – and poor circulation. The counter argument to this is that once you start exercising, blood begins to flow freely through the limbs, slowing down the digestive process and promoting movement.

THE FIRST PERSON TO SWIM THE ENGLISH CHANNEL WAS CAPTAIN WEBB IN 1875. MISS GERTRUDE EDERLE, A BUTCHER'S DAUGHTER FROM NEW YORK, WAS THE FIRST WOMAN TO ACCOMPLISH THE FEAT, IN 1926. SHE LEARNT TO SWIM AFTER NEARLY DROWNING IN A LAKE IN GERMANY AT THE AGE OF SEVEN. SHE DIED IN 2003 AT THE AGE OF 98.

If cramp does strike while you're swimming, you need to get back on land as quickly as possible and stretch the affected limb – or get someone to do it for you. Try to float on your back, breathe in deeply, and paddle with your arms for buoyancy and to manoeuvre yourself to safety. The advice of Dr Franklin, contributor to the 1890s bestseller *Enquire Within*, was: 'When he [the swimmer] is seized by the cramp, the method of driving it away is to give the parts affected a sudden, vigorous and violent shock; which he may do in the air as he swims on his back.'

IN 1927 THE *GIRL GUIDES' MANUAL* DECLARED BRITISH GIRLS TO BE WELL BEHIND THEIR CONTEMPORARIES IN NORWAY AND SWEDEN, OF LITTLE 'REAL USE' UNTIL THEY COULD SWIM, AND THAT '...TO LEARN SWIMMING IS NO MORE DIFFICULT THAN TO LEARN BICYCLING'.

EAT YOUR GREENS

Unfortunately for reluctant children – and adults too – greens really do you good. So do vegetables in any other colour. Eat them and you have a good chance of keeping healthy for life.

The substances in vegetables that pack the most powerful punch are the antioxidants, which include vitamin C, lycopene – contained in red fruits like tomatoes – and beta-carotene, the substance that makes carrots and sweet potatoes orange.

In their normal day-to-day metabolism, cells release free radicals, including unstable oxygen molecules that antioxidants mop up. Left unchecked, free radicals can damage body cells (a possible precursor of cancer) and contribute to the build-up of the fatty deposits in the arteries that can cause heart disease and strokes.

There's more. Vegetables contain fibre to help keep you regular. Beans and peas are especially useful as they contain soluble, easily absorbed fibre. Fresh or frozen, they can help the health of everything from your eyesight to your immune system.

Incidentally...

Maybe you can't help disliking green vegetables. Some 20–25 per cent of us are 'supertasters', with taste buds genetically programmed to be so sensitive to the bitter chemicals in vegetables (especially brassicas) that they simply can't tolerate them. However, these nasty tasting substances are believed to have anti-cancer properties.

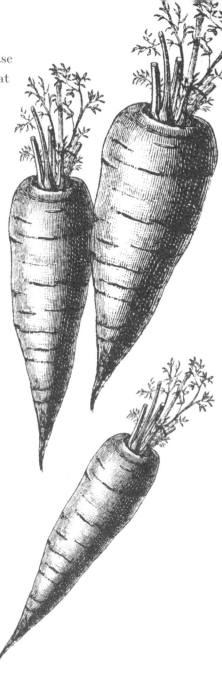

According to the anonymous nonsense rhyme:
I eat my peas with honey,
I've done it all my life.
It makes the peas taste funny
But it keeps them on my knife.

SUCKED THUMB, CROOKED TEETH

S o it was said, but because babies lose their first or milk teeth, this is only a problem in children who carry on sucking their thumbs after their adult teeth begin to erupt, from the age of about six.

Sucking is babies' essential response to ensure they get the food they need. It is also perfectly natural – ultrasound scans sometimes reveal babies sucking their thumbs even while still in the womb. It is also pleasurable and, for young babies, a good way of exploring their mouths.

The pleasure persists: as they grow older, babies suck their thumbs when they are tired or when they need to relax. What worries parents is the persistence of this habit into childhood, and that it may be a sign of insecurity. Today's childcare experts largely agree that the time to worry — and to take action to find the

A cautionary tale

The strictures of Victorian and Edwardian upbringing outlawed thumb sucking, especially in older children. Many a child has been terrified by 'The Story of Little Suck-a-Thumb', a cautionary poem from *Struwwelpeter*, published in 1903. In the poem, Conrad, though warned against it by his mother, sucks his thumb while she is out. This is what happens next:

The door flew open, in he ran,

The great red-legged scissor-man.

Oh! Children see! The tailor's come

And caught out little Suck-a-Thumb.

Snip! Snap! Snip! The scissors go;

And Conrad cries out 'Oh! Oh! Oh!'

Snip! Snap! Snip! They go so fast,

That both his thumbs are off at last.

Mamma comes home: there Conrad stands,

And looks quite sad, and shows his hands;

'Ah!' said Mamma, 'I knew he'd come

To naughty little Suck-a-Thumb.'

underlying cause – is if a child prefers sucking their thumb to playing or interacting with others, or if the habit persists for so long that adult teeth are starting to become misaligned.

DON'T RUN
BEFORE YOU CAN WALK

A plea for patience, and a proverb that mirrors the natural progression of babies from toddlers to fully mobile youngsters because, of course, practice makes perfect.

Walking upright on two legs – the uniquely human stance – is a skill that most children acquire sometime around their first birthday. Babies who are fast, expert crawlers are often reluctant to persevere with walking, but they get there in the end, as well as learning to walk on tiptoe, jump and skip.

When babies start to walk their natural balance-aiding stance is wide and bow legged. After the age of two this usually disappears quite naturally. Today's children rarely have the permanent bowing associated with rickets: this softening and bending of the bones is caused by lack of vitamin D, which needs for its formation both sunshine and a diet rich in fatty fish (or a cod liver oil supplement). Young sufferers would, in the past, spend several years with their legs in splints until the problem was rectified.

IT IS ESTIMATED THAT THE BUSHMAN CHILDREN OF THE KALAHARI ARE CARRIED OVER 4,500 MILES (7,200KM) BY THEIR MOTHERS BEFORE THEY BEGIN TO WALK.

It's rude to point

So say the books of etiquette, because pointing is conspicuous and unpleasant, drawing undue attention to both the pointer and their unfortunate object.

Miss Manners, the American guru, advises her 'Gentle Reader' thus: 'The unpleasantness of being pointed at applies not only to strangers at a distance but also, you will be surprised to hear, to close-by acquaintances shouting "the error is yours!" '

The pointing finger has other associations, too. In World War I the extended digit of Lord Kitchener, pictured with the words 'Britons [Kitchener] Wants You' and the exhortation 'Join Your Country's Army!' helped recruit 2.5 million men in the first year and a half of the war, many thousands of them destined to die.

In the USA, too, Uncle Sam pointed the finger. 'I want you for US Army' was the original recruiting slogan of 1917, and it was used again to boost recruitment after the USA

Incidentally...

Pointing can be an attribute in the animal world. A Pointer is a gundog bred and trained to stand rigid when it scents game (such as pheasant, partridge and quail) killed by a huntsman and to point to it with its nose. The dog's tail, which is naturally held straight and level with the back, adds to this streamlined, pointing effect.

joined World War II following the attack on Pearl Harbor in December 1941. According to legend, Uncle Sam was developed as an interpretation of the 'US' stamped on barrels of rations supplied to the US Army in the war of 1812 by a meatpacker named 'Uncle' Sam Wilson.

EAT BREAD AND BUTTER BEFORE CAKE

The golden rule of the nursery was an admonition against greed at the tea table, especially for children. Equally, for frugal parents, it was a way of ensuring that hungry offspring satiated their appetites with inexpensive bread and viewed cakes as a treat.

Tea was originally a meal served before bed because, until the 19th century, dinner was eaten at midday, supper in the early evening and tea was the last meal of the day. As more men began to work outside the home, supper became later and later and eventually tea was a meal that filled the afternoon gap between luncheon and dinner, or sustained children after their school work was completed and office workers when they arrived home.

The 'polite' middle-class tea consisted of small sandwiches and cakes, but for working class families it contained eggs, meat or both. As well as eating their bread or toast first, well-mannered children, when it was time for cake, would be expected to 'take the first that comes' rather than reaching across a serving plate for the delicacy they fancied most.

Taking tea in the afternoon also became popular in the USA in the 19th century, with five o'clock the most popular hour. The American housewife was advised not to omit 'the porcelain platters bearing wafer-like slices of buttered bread, cakelets, and, if you would be thoroughly English, a shape of hot buttered bread...'

ALLOWING CHILDREN TO INDULGE THEMSELVES ON 'FANCY' FOOD OF ANY KIND – AND EVEN JAM AS WELL AS BUTTER ON BREAD – WAS PARTICULARLY FROWNED UPON IN THE VICTORIAN ERA. 'WE LEARN FROM DAILY EXPERIENCE,' SAID *ENQUIRE WITHIN*, 'THAT THE LEAST INDULGED THRIVE MUCH BETTER, UNFOLD ALL THEIR FACULTIES QUICKER AND ACQUIRE MORE MUSCULAR STRENGTH AND VIGOUR OF MIND THAN THOSE THAT ARE CONSTANTLY FAVOURED...'

DON'T EAT BETWEEN MEALS

When mealtimes were strictly kept, and children pressured to clear their plates, eating between meals was frowned on because it dulled the appetite. And in many weight-control regimes, snacking is regarded as a sure way of breaking the diet.

Incidentally...

For children sent away to boarding school the tuck box was a welcome supplement to the school diet and from the 1750s the word 'tuck' became synonymous with food. Schools also had tuck shops selling sweets, cakes and other treats.

The truth is, whether eating between meals is healthy or not all depends on what you eat, how much and in what context. Stuffing yourself with high-fat, high-salt, high-carbohydrate snacks can be a sure way of piling on the weight, like one 33-stone (210kg), 6ft 6in (1.95m) 17-year-old who confessed to snacking daily on sweets, biscuits, cakes and crisps between meals and late at night. By contrast, if you are on a low-calorie diet, eating two small 100-calorie snacks a day between main meals not only helps to stave off hunger pangs but keeps your blood sugar levels constant, putting less strain on your pancreas, the organ that secretes the hormone insulin, vital to sugar metabolism.

In Britain, schools were permitted by the 1926 Education (Provision of Meals) Act to provide free or low-cost meals for schoolchildren and a daily bottle of milk. This measure alone helped to reduce child mortality rates considerably.

KEEP YOUR ELBOWS
OFF THE TABLE

O r, as grandmother used to warn, 'all joints on the table will be carved'. Yet another of the old rules once sternly enforced on children, to their dread. Particularly undesirable, say the etiquette police, is to sit with the left elbow on the table while eating with the right hand, or while lifting a glass.

For leaning forward in animated after-dinner conversation, it is said, resting on the elbows is perfectly permissible. But Miss Manners, in her *Ultimate Handbook on Modern Etiquette*, maintains that 'Elbows are banned during eating because of the awkward, crane like motion it gives to the hand on the other end of the elbow… Also it is a delightfully easy error to catch children in, whose other errors may be more subtle.'

A PRACTICAL JOKE ONCE COMMON IN FACTORIES AND OTHER WORKPLACES WAS FOR THE NEWEST APPRENTICE OR GREENHORN TO BE SENT OUT TO BUY A CAN OF 'ELBOW GREASE'. THIS, OF COURSE, IS MERELY AN EXPRESSION FOR VIGOROUS WORK.

The elbow — the joint which, together with the shoulder, gives the arm its mobility, and when bent allows us distance from our neighbour — is actually composed of two joints. The major joint is the hinge where the two forearm bones, the radius and the ulna, meet the humerus, the bone of the upper arm. At the second, the superior radio-ulnar joint, the top of the radius articulates with a notch in the adjacent ulna, allowing the arm to pivot.

CHEESE GIVES YOU NIGHTMARES

Not just a piece of everyday health guidance on late evening eating, but a link with ancient medical practice and legends linking cheese with witchcraft.

To avoid nightmares, the accepted advice is that any food that is hard to digest should be shunned at bedtime. This was the belief of the Greek physician Galen. Those prone to nightmares should also, it was said, take their last meal at least three hours before sleeping and avoid doing mental work for the same period.

According to modern science, the problems with cheese stem from the chemical tyramine, which is made by bacteria in cheese. Tyramine not only raises the blood pressure — a stress symptom associated with nightmares — but can, in susceptible people, alter the activity of nerves in the brain and bring on migraines.

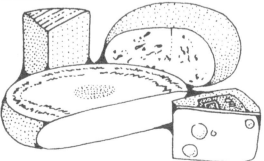

Incidentally…

According to legend, witches sit on people's bellies at night, rendering their victims breathless and unable to cry out or use their hands to push the evil away, and leaving their victims exhausted in the morning. Witches, who with magic bridles changed people into horses (hence the 'mare' in nightmare), were also thought of as cheese women, who would tempt men into adultery while they slept.

Children's nightmares usually begin when, at about the age of four, their imaginations start to develop. And while much of the old advice still holds good – never speak impatiently to a child who wakes in fear; leave a light on for a child who dreads the dark; avoid overstimulation and creepy stories at night; talk through and 'exorcise' the dream – parents today, unlike their counterparts of a century ago, are unlikely to think of constipation or 'faulty feeding' as nightmares' primary cause.

DON'T SQUEEZE SPOTS, THEY'LL TURN SEPTIC

Squeezing spots is an easy way of introducing bacteria that can exacerbate the problem, delay healing and even leave scars. But it is a myth that full-blown acne can be caused by spot squeezing, lack of washing or eating chocolate.

Spots erupt when sebum, the skin's oily secretion, blocks the pores. As a result, blackheads form and bacteria may proliferate, causing pus-filled pimples. These are the scourge of adolescence because this is the time when, under

MANY DISEASES, SUCH AS CHICKENPOX, ERUPT IN CHARACTERISTIC TYPES OF SPOTS. POCK AND POX ARE OLD WORDS FOR SPOTS, PARTICULARLY ASSOCIATED WITH THE DEADLY SMALLPOX, WHICH, THANKS TO VACCINATION THROUGHOUT THE 19TH AND 20TH CENTURIES, WAS CERTIFIED AS ERADICATED WORLDWIDE IN 1977.

hormonal influence, the sebaceous glands generate additional sebum production. In severe acne, the blocked pores may develop into hard cysts which, when they eventually disappear, leave pits in the skin. True acne needs medical attention – for both physical and psychological reasons – but home treatment to rid the skin of excess oil can help the teenager who gets the occasional spot.

Tea tree oil is a long-used aboriginal treatment for spots. It has anti-inflammatory and antibacterial effects and has been shown to be fairly successful in the treatment of acne. Great burdock is an old English country remedy, and recent experiments have shown that burdock root (available from herbalists in capsule form) contains substances that help to kill both bacteria and fungi.

Beauty spots or marks are flat, dark moles on the face, usually near the mouth or eyes, that are considered to enhance the looks rather than detract from them. False beauty spots, detachable black patches, which were sometimes cut out in fancy shapes such as stars or hearts, were once worn by women and the most foppish men, and reached the height of their popularity in the Regency period of the early 19th century. The fashion for beauty spots was revived in the mid-20th century.

Count sheep
to fall asleep

The age-old remedy for getting to sleep is only one of many strategies for nodding off. It is the rhythm and monotony of sheep-counting that is believed to help the brain change its electrical rhythms from the pattern typical of wakefulness into that of sleep.

If this doesn't work, there are lots of other angles to try, like 'taking a walk' around a favourite place or telling yourself a bedtime story. The trick is to help the brain to turn off its customary 'noise' so that you forget your everyday worries and fall asleep. If all that fails, then get up and do something useful.

SHEPHERDS IN THE NORTH OF ENGLAND HAVE THEIR OWN ANCIENT NUMBERING SYSTEM FOR COUNTING SHEEP; THERE ARE MANY LOCAL VARIATIONS, BUT ONE VERSION, FROM ONE TO TEN, RUNS: YAN, TAN, TETHERA, PETHERA, PIMP, SETHERA, METHERA, HOVERA, COVERA, DIK.

No rest

The causes of unwanted wakefulness are many and varied. The long list contained in the *Concise Household Encyclopedia* of 1933 still holds good today:

- Cold feet
- Bad ventilation of the bedroom
- Uncomfortable bed, too heavy, too warm, or insufficient bedclothing
- A hot room
- Hunger or a full stomach
- Too high or too low a pillow
- Noise

- Too much light in the room
- Tea or coffee taken late in the evening
- Mental or physical overwork and exhaustion
- Want of exercise
- Worry, financial anxiety, domestic troubles
- Retiring at irregular hours, and… many other small errors that can be corrected

Incidentally…

Herbs of all kinds have long been used in remedies for insomnia, including a pillow filled with hops, lavender or valerian root. A traditional 'slumber tea' for children was made from an infusion of valerian root, dried lemon balm, chamomile leaves, bitter orange blossom and rosehips, sweetened with honey.

BREAST IS BEST

Not just because breast milk is the natural food for babies but also because it imparts some immunity against disease. What's more, it is believed to lower the risks of high blood pressure, heart disease and strokes in later life.

The fluid that flows
from a new mother's breasts in the
first 72 hours after giving birth is colostrum,
which is rich in infection-fighting antibodies that
prevent intestinal infections. It also contains a substance

that produces an insulin-like growth factor, which helps to stimulate muscle growth.

The nutritious sugars in breast milk (oligosaccharides) are also thought to kill harmful bacteria – notably food poisoning bacteria such as *E. coli* – and to promote the proliferation of 'friendly' bacteria in the gut, which may boost the immune system and improve babies' resistance to allergies. The substances that help maintain a healthy blood pressure in adults who were breast-fed as babies are long-chain polyunsaturated fatty acids, which are components of the fats in human milk. The precise composition of the milk varies from day to day, depending on the mother's diet and other factors.

Before the arrival of 'formula', a wet nurse was the only solution for women unable to breast-feed, and for orphans, although the upper classes employed wet nurses for social reasons – Queen Victoria described breast-feeding as 'making a cow of oneself'. Wet nurses were chosen with care; brunettes were preferred to blondes or redheads because their milk was considered to be more nutritious and their temperaments more 'balanced'.

Incidentally…

Babies have been fed from cups and bottles from ancient times, containers being made from materials as diverse as cows' horns, terracotta, leather and pewter. Milk from donkeys (thought to be healthy because it looked most like human milk), mares and goats was used, as well as cows' milk, but infection, especially from unsterilized containers, is more likely to have been a problem than malnutrition.

Drink a pint
of milk a day

An expression that entered the language in 1959 in an advertisement from Britain's Dairy Council, this is still sound advice, though adults wanting to consume plenty of calcium but less animal fat should choose their milk with care.

It is a neat coincidence that a pint (600ml) of whole milk contains about 700mg of calcium, the daily recommended intake for adults and young children, though teenagers and nursing mothers need more – 800 to 1,000mg. Calcium is the mineral needed to build strong bones – and to help prevent osteoporosis later in life.

Before milk was routinely pasteurized prior to distribution, by heating it to a high temperature to kill any bacteria it might contain – and before children were immunized against killer infections – it was often the vehicle by which diseases including diphtheria, tuberculosis (consumption) and typhoid were transmitted. Parents were urged to boil milk if there was any danger of contamination.

GOOD NEWS FOR SLIMMERS: RECENT STUDIES HAVE SHOWN THAT THE CALCIUM IN MILK NOT ONLY STIMULATES THE BODY TO BURN MORE FAT BUT HELPS REDUCE THE AMOUNT OF NEW FAT THE BODY IS CAPABLE OF MAKING.

DON'T WEAR WOOL NEXT TO YOUR SKIN

This is good advice for those with sensitive skins, though in the past, when winters – and homes – were much colder than today, woollen underclothes were undoubtedly the best way of keeping warm.

Woollens keep us snug by trapping a thick layer of insulating air in their natural fibres, and do so much more effectively than silk or cotton. They also absorb a great deal of moisture without feeling damp. As wool absorbs water it also gives off heat, making the wearer feel even warmer.

The downside of wearing wool is that its fibres can irritate the skin, causing itching and irritation. However, it may not always be the wool itself that is entirely to blame, but the substance it has been washed in. Even mild detergents specially formulated for washing wool can provoke unfavourable reactions in some people. The good news is that modern artificial fibres come close to imitating wool's warming properties without its propensity for irritating the skin.

The health benefits of wool for undergarments that allow the skin to 'breathe' were first recognized in the 1880s by health gurus such as the German doctor Gustav Jaeger, and woollen combinations soon became standard wear.

SIGNS OF
NATURE

The closeness between countless generations of humans and the natural world is expressed in the many sayings that relate to plants and animals – and to the weather. In times past, extraordinary weather phenomena were attributed to the whims of deities, and weather perfectly suited to the needs of farmers and fishermen was a sign of the gods' good grace.

Long before Admiral Robert Fitzroy, then the Superintendent of Britain's Meteorological Office, coined the phrase 'weather forecast' in August 1861, farmers, sailors and country folk had been looking skyward to foretell the weather. The Greeks started the science of meteorology, relating day-to-day weather to the direction of the wind. The first rules of weather forecasting are enshrined in *On Weather Signs* written in the 4th century BC by Aristotle and his pupil Theophrastus.

That many (though by no means all) of the sayings about the natural world still hold true today is testament to our ancestors' powers of observation. That so many relate to Christian festivals and rites of passage such as marriage and death also underlines the strength of the links between our lives and the natural round.

RING ROUND THE MOON, SNOW SOON

In winter, it may quite possibly be so. Or the ring could be a sign that rain is on the way, depending on how cold it is. But it needs to be the right kind of ring.

On a winter's night a pale ring or halo around the moon – shimmering with faint rainbow colours, with the red on the inside – is a magnificent sight, often more spectacular because many of the stars are blotted out by cloud. Sometimes it lasts for only a few minutes, but if it persists for longer you may see the different colours strengthen and fade as the ice crystals move about, turning and swirling in the cloud.

Comprising the moon's halo are millions of minute, hexagonal ice crystals, often borne on moisture-laden cirrostratus cloud. In its infancy, this cloud is thin and high enough – about 22,000ft (6,000m) above the ground – to be penetrated by the sun's rays illuminating the moon from below the horizon. We see a halo because each of the ice crystals bends the sun's light twice. If the cloud then thickens and lowers, snow or rain will almost certainly fall. If the cloud disperses then it won't.

Incidentally…

Shepherds and sailors have long believed that a new moon on a Saturday or a full one on a Sunday foretell bad weather. The combination occurring in succession is considered to be the worst of both worlds.

Just to confuse, there is another phenomenon, the corona, which invariably includes a brownish ring, with bluish-white colours towards the inside. If red is there at all it will be to the outside. Because it is formed by sunlight passing through a general dispersal of water droplets in the atmosphere, not ice in clouds, a corona round the moon has nothing to do with foretelling the weather.

Halos form around the sun in exactly the same way as those around the moon, but it is dangerous to look at them directly. They, too, are good predictors of rain.

WHEN SWALLOWS FLY LOW, RAIN IS ON THE WAY

Although swallows rarely fly very high in the sky, these graceful birds have been used as weather predictors since ancient times.

The Roman poet Virgil was one of the earliest recorders of typical swallow behaviour:

Wet weather seldom hurts the most unwise;
So plain the signs, such prophets are the skies.
The swallow skims the river's watery face;
The frogs renew the croaks of their loquacious race.

To have swallows or martins nesting in your eaves is a sign of both luck and wealth. But to rob a swallow's nest is so bad that, say the traditional pessimists, it will taint cows' milk with blood.

On a fine day, as they hunt for flying insects, swallows will alternately glide high in the air to catch groups of weak prey, drawn up from the ground by warm air currents, and swoop down lower over open ground or water, where large insects abound. But when the air pressure falls and the air is full of moisture (whether or not it is going to rain) insects descend much closer to the ground, and therefore so do the swallows that pursue them.

When it's wet and windy, insects go to ground or stay lodged in vegetation or in the lee of a hedge or wall. Then the swallows have to travel farther from their nests – to places such as rivers or sewage farms – and will sometimes pick insects off tree leaves or even forage for food on the ground. Near the coast, especially when it's windy, you can see swallows feeding low on the wing on sandhoppers and flies.

WHEN GORSE IS OUT OF BLOOM, KISSING'S OUT OF FASHION

This English country saying acknowledges the fact that gorse can be seen in flower throughout the year – and possibly also refers to the prevalence of gorse in the open spaces that are lovers' traditional meeting places.

The botanical key to this saying is that, in England and Wales, different species of gorse – all with bright yellow pea-like flowers and a wonderfully heady scent – grow close together. In a mild year the common gorse (*Ulex europaeus*) flowers from late winter to mid-summer, then two rarer species come into flower for the rest of the year: the western gorse (*U. gallii*), which grows on acid,

Incidentally…

Country gardeners still use gorse for
keeping rodents and other pests off
pea and bean seedlings.

western moors, and, in the south
and east of England, the dwarf or
lesser gorse (*U. minor*).

It is said that Carolus Linnaeus,
the Swedish botanist who devised the
system of plant classification, fell to his
knees in wonder when he first saw gorse in bloom.
The location was probably Putney Heath, near London; the year,
1736. Gorse, like its close relation the broom, has had many domestic uses,
from fuel to cattle fodder, and for sweeping anything from floors to chimneys.

Cats will always find their way home

There is plenty of proof that this is true, and some cats
have journeys of thousands of miles on record. But it is
an old wives' tale that putting butter on a cat's paws will
stop it wandering away after a house move.

In 1981, records *The Guinness Book of Oddities*, a Turk named Mehmet Tunc
was on a journey from Germany with his cat Minosch. When they reached

the Turkish border the cat disappeared, only to turn up 61 days later 1,500 miles (2,400km) away at the Tunc family home back in Germany. Another cat, named Sugar, despite being hampered by a deformed hip, even crossed the Rockies, at the rate of 100 miles (160km) a month, to be reunited with her owners who had moved from Anderson, California to Gage, Oklahoma, a place she had never visited before.

Cats find their way, it is thought, by using the sun as both a compass and a clock. Like migratory birds they may also be able to detect subtle changes in the earth's magnetic field. Once they get nearer to home, they use their sense of smell which, as in humans, has a strong link to the memory.

Incidentally

Wherever they live, cats establish a home territory for themselves in which smell memories are crucial. If this overlaps with the territory of a neighbouring cat, the two animals will commonly avoid each other by using different paths or by going outdoors at different times of the day or night.

DOGS CAN SMELL STRANGERS

Except for identical twins who, because our odours are inherited, share exactly the same smell, molecule for molecule, dogs can easily detect the difference between individuals. The record breakers are bloodhounds, which have been known to follow trails several days old, or stretching 100 miles (160km) and more.

Dogs have a sense of smell that is vastly superior to that of humans. This has much to do with the size and composition of their olfactory epithelium, the sheet of tissue at the top of the nasal cavity that is sensitive to aromas. This is twenty times bigger in dogs than it is in humans and is supplied with more than a hundred times as many smell-sensitive cells.

Dogs are particularly good at detecting the substances that comprise human sweat, notably butyric acid, and it is this that makes them so good at finding the buried victims of avalanches and earthquakes. This ability is proved in the pebble test. Six people

Beware of being followed by a strange dog – it's said to be an omen of ill fortune.

each pick up a pebble and throw it as far as they can. The dog then sniffs the hand of one person and will successfully retrieve the pebble thrown by them.

In the wild, dogs use smell as a vital means of finding food located a long way off, for enhancing the strength of the pack and for finding a mate. The reason why dogs occasionally roll in cow or horse dung may be to disguise their smell from rabbits and other potential live food. It may also be a signal for members of the pack to gather round before a hunt.

DOG DAYS, THE PERIOD BETWEEN 3 JULY AND 11 AUGUST, GET THEIR NAME FROM THE ROMANS' BELIEF THAT THE HEAT OF HIGH SUMMER, WHICH THEY CALLED *CANICULARES DIES*, WAS CAUSED BY THE DOG STAR SIRIUS RISING WITH THE SUN.

COWS LIE DOWN WHEN IT'S GOING TO RAIN

They do – and they don't! In other words they are poor weather forecasters, though some farmers claim that cows predict storms by exhibiting bad-tempered behaviour. Cows with any sense will shelter from a downpour by standing or lying down under nearby trees.

Animal rain lore

Many other animal behaviours are erroneously used to forecast rain. So, don't bank on rain if…

A pigeon washes

A sparrow chirps

A cat washes over its ears

A robin comes near the house

Geese wander

A chicken rolls in the dust

The truth about cow behaviour is that, rain or shine, they generally stand up to eat in the morning and evening and lie down – for anything up to 12 hours – to chew the cud during the rest of the day or night. Being herd animals, what one does, all (or most) do, so when you pass a field of cows you are very likely to see them all eating or all chewing.

Cattle chew the cud to get maximum benefit from hard-to-digest grass. A cow's stomach has four compartments, which are used in a specific order. Ingested grass enters the large first stomach, where it is softened and overflows into the smaller second stomach. From both first and second stomachs food is regurgitated in small portions – or cuds – and ruminated. It is then swallowed into the third stomach and finally into the fourth or 'true' stomach, from where it goes on into the intestine.

RAIN BEFORE SEVEN, FINE BY ELEVEN

A good forecast in many temperate locations, as long as you are liberal enough to take 'seven' and 'eleven' to mean early and late morning. It is certainly more reliable than its counterpart 'fine before seven, rain by eleven'.

This saying works because the weather that accompanies a depression is unlikely to last more than four to eight hours, and rainfall that begins the previous night is likely to peter out before noon the next day. A depression or low pressure area is formed when masses of cold and warm air meet and the warm air rises over the cold. As a result, clouds develop and rain falls. If the pressure falls even more it becomes windy as air is sucked in because, as in the school rhyme: 'winds always blow from high to low [pressure].'

On average a raindrop measures 1/12in (2mm) across.

Raindrops, technically 'precipitation that reaches the ground in liquid form', result from the collision of droplets inside a turbulent cloud, making them large enough to fall to the ground. Alternatively, when supercooled water droplets and ice crystals exist together in a cloud, water droplets move towards and enlarge the ice crystals until they are large enough to fall. Whether they reach the ground as rain, sleet or snow depends on air temperature.

According to a rhyme said to be by the 19th-century judge Baron Charles Bowen:

The rain it raineth every day
Upon the Just and Unjust fella,
But more upon the Just because
The unjust stole the Just's umbrella.

RED SKY AT NIGHT, SHEPHERD'S DELIGHT

… red sky in the morning, shepherd's (or sailor's) warning.' Wherever the weather comes predominantly from the west, the first part of this saying is one of the most reliable traditional weather forecasts, as long as you can distinguish a benign red sky from a livid, angry one.

The colours in the sky arise from the dust and moisture in the atmosphere, which split and scatter the sun's light. At the beginning and end of the day, when sunlight has to travel farthest, the 'long' red, orange and yellow rays of the spectrum are scattered least, and are therefore most visible. If, as the sun sets, the sky glows rosy pink, this signals dry air in the west, from where the next day's weather will arrive. Moisture in the atmosphere makes the light disperse differently, creating the vivid yellow or reddish-orange clouds that predict rain.

In the morning, a yellow sky also forecasts rain. If it is red, then the chance of rain depends on the type of

The saying is only applicable as a weather prediction in the middle latitudes, where most storm systems move from west to east. Nearer the poles the sun rises and sets too far from east and west, and in the tropics winds blow from the east.

clouds and their extent. As the 19th-century forecaster CL Prince observed: 'If at sunrise small reddish-looking clouds are seen low on the horizon, it must not always be considered to indicate rain... It has frequently been observed that if [the clouds] extend ten degrees, rain will follow before two or three pm; but if still higher and nearer the zenith [the point directly above an observer], rain will fall within three hours.'

VERY RARELY, AND MOST PROBABLY OVER THE OCEAN AT HIGH LATITUDES, YOU MAY SEE A GREEN FLASH AT THE MOMENT THE SUN DISAPPEARS AT SUNSET OR RISES AT DAWN. AT SUCH PROPITIOUS MOMENTS IT IS SAID THAT YOU SHOULD MAKE A WISH.

Other good early morning predictions

For a rain-free day:

Clouds driven away by the sunrise.
Grey sky to the east.
A sea that looks darker than the sky.

For rain to come:

Dark clouds in the west.
Too bright a sky.
A red sky, with the sun rising over
a bank of cloud (a high dawn).

Don't eat wild BLACKBERRIES AFTER MICHAELMAS

Because, according to legend, on Michaelmas night, 29 September, the feast of St Michael the Archangel, the Devil spits or urinates on them. Certainly blackberries begin to lose their flavour at this time, when they are also likely to get damp and mouldy or be affected by early frosts.

Seeds that have been discovered by archaeologists in the stomachs of Neolithic human remains prove that Britons have been enjoying the juicy purple fruits of the blackberry (*Rubus fruticosus*) for over 4,000 years. And since medieval times blackberry leaves, infused in boiling water and honey, have been valued for treating inflammation of the mouth, and to soothe both digestive ills and the pain of gout.

Sometimes known as 'lawyers' because their thorny, arching stems are difficult to escape from once they entrap you, brambles were also

Incidentally...

Old recipes for blackberries include blackberry crowdie, made with oats, cream and rum, and bramble jelly. Paired with apples, they are the perfect ingredient for an autumn pie or crumble.

commonly planted around graves, for the practical reason of deterring sheep and weeds; also to keep the dead in their place and the Devil out.

Never smile
at a crocodile

And don't get near one either — they can be deadly. Camouflaged to look like floating logs, with only their eyes and nostrils visible above the surface of the water, crocs lurk in the shallows waiting to sense the smells and vibrations of nearby prey.

The song in which this phrase was coined was written in 1952 by Jack Lawrence and Frank Churchill for the Walt Disney movie version of *Peter Pan*, which was released the following year. The first verse goes:

> *Never smile at a crocodile,*
> *No you can't get friendly with a crocodile,*
> *Don't be taken in by his welcome grin,*
> *He's imagining how well you'll fit within his skin.*

Incidentally...

'Crocodile tears', which stream from the reptiles' eyes, are thought to be the way they rid themselves of excess salt. It was once believed that crocodiles used them, along with moaning sounds, to attract sympathy — and victims — hence their association with hypocrisy.

In the story, the crocodile — which ticked because it had swallowed a clock — terrorizes the villainous Captain Hook.

A crocodile strikes with sudden, awesome power, instinctively shaking its prey from side to side. Experts say that playing dead, which can prompt the animal to leave its victim under rocks or logs to eat later, provides a slim likelihood of surviving an attack. Poking the creature in the eye or pulling its tail are other last resorts.

In a real life horror story, Brett Mann, a 22-year-old Australian, was killed by a saltwater crocodile after being swept away by the current in the Finniss River in December 2003. His two teenage companions managed to swim to, then climb, a tree where they stayed until rescued by helicopter, while the croc stalked beneath them, hopeful of another meal.

To tell crocodiles and alligators apart, look at the teeth: in a crocodile at least one tooth is visible at the side of the head when the mouth is shut. Crocodiles — unlike alligators which, apart from the rare Chinese alligator, live only in North and South America — inhabit tropical regions throughout the world.

ON MAGPIES: ONE FOR SORROW, TWO FOR MIRTH

The magpie, with its striking black and white plumage and long tail, has long been a bird of ill omen. Its colouring is said by many to have come from its refusal to take on full black mourning after Christ's crucifixion.

According to long-held superstition, whether ill luck – or some other life-changing event – will befall you depends on how many magpies you see together. A more upbeat version begins:

One for sorrow, two for joy,
Three for a girl and four for a boy.

Or alternatively (though there are several more versions):

Three for a wedding, four for death,
Five for silver, six for gold,
Seven for a secret, not to be told,
Eight for heaven, nine for—[Hell],
And ten for the D...l's own sell.

Magpies will peck at windows, thinking that their own reflections are rival birds.

There are many traditional ways of dispelling the ill luck of seeing a single magpie. You should, some believe, bow and say aloud: 'Good morning to you Mr Magpie, Sir,' or, 'Good magpie, magpie, chatter and flee, turn up thy tail

Incidentally...

Young magpies, probably in search of mates, gather in treetop groups which in winter can be 20 or even 40 strong. These gatherings are known as parliaments, probably from their raucous 'chak-chak-chakking' in chorus, like roused politicians.

and good luck fall me.' Others make great ceremony of removing their hats when a single magpie crosses their path; yet others will spit or make the sign of the cross on the ground.

The magpie (*Pica pica*) is a close relative of the crow and breeds all over Europe, except for Iceland. It is increasingly common near human habitations, where it supplements its insect and grain diet with food scraps. The magpie's reputation for stealing is immortalized in Rossini's opera *La Gazza Ladra* (*The Thieving Magpie*) of 1817, in which a maidservant is condemned to death for the bird's crime.

A CUCKOO IN SEPTEMBER, NO ONE EVER CAN REMEMBER

A tribute to the migratory habits of the cuckoo, though in some country districts people once believed that in the autumn cuckoos changed into hawks in order to survive the British winter. In years gone by, contributors to the letters page of *The Times* would vie closely to be the first to report hearing the first cuckoo of spring – by tradition a lucky event.

This saying is the last line of a rhyme with several versions, one of which is:

Cuckoo, cuckoo, pray what do you do?
In April [Ap-er-il] *I open my bill*
In May I sing both night and noon
In June I change my tune
In July away I fly
In August away I must.

As the rhyme rightly relates, the call of the cuckoo (*Cuculus canorus*) is most persistent in early summer, then it changes subtly to a 'cuk-cuck-oo' later in the season. The cuckoo is renowned as a brood parasite, laying its huge eggs in the nest of small birds, including meadow pipits and hedge sparrows. The eggs hatch into large young, which evict the rest of the clutch. Their massive gapes are irresistible to the rearing instincts of the foster parents, which spend from 17 to 21 exhausting days bringing food.

Unlike the parasitical cuckoos of Eurasia, America's yellow-billed cuckoos build their own nests in which to lay their eggs, though sometimes the female will lay in the nest of another cuckoo.

Cuckoo lore

Like magpies, cuckoos are the object of many superstitions:

The number of consecutive calls you hear is the number of years until you marry.

If you hear a cuckoo before the swallows have arrived, sorrow lies ahead for you.

When you hear the first cuckoo, look under your shoe. You will find a hair the same colour as that of your spouse-to-be.

Whatever you are doing when you hear the first cuckoo you will continue to do all year.

The luckiest time to hear a first cuckoo is on Easter morning.

If you have money in your pocket when you hear the first cuckoo then you will have wealth all year.

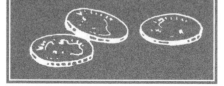

CUCKOO SPIT (ALSO KNOWN AS FROG SPIT) IS THE FROTHY WHITE EXUDATE DEPOSITED ON PLANT LEAVES BY INSECTS, ESPECIALLY THOSE OF THE FROGHOPPER FAMILY CERCOPIDAE, TO PROTECT THEIR LARVAE.

HORSES SLEEP STANDING UP

They do – although they sleep lying down as well. This ability to stand and 'power nap' allows horses to get the rest they need and to make a quick escape from predators if necessary.

Horses are able to doze standing up because they possess a stay apparatus – a system of ligaments and tendons that holds the creatures in a standing position while their muscles relax. They will spend 4–15 hours a day in 'standing rest', while taking short naps totalling about two hours.

Incidentally...

The practice of shoeing horses began around 200 BC. Hanging a horseshoe at the threshold of your house or on a ship's mast is said to keep away witches and evil spirits – but only if you make sure that the open end is upwards. This way, the good luck won't fall out.

Like humans, horses experience sleep of different kinds. Their standing or slow wave sleep (named from brainwave frequency) is a shallow sleep. Only when they lie down can horses experience rapid eye movement (REM) sleep – the equivalent of our dreaming sleep. A horse needs comparatively little of this type of sleep, probably an hour or two a week, but without it is likely to become ill-tempered or neurotic.

Studies of horses show that they have more REM sleep when they live in groups, because one horse will stand sentinel while others relax in safety. Even in a comfortable stable a horse may feel isolated, confined – and wakeful – especially if it fears becoming 'cast': trapped against a wall with insufficient room to get to its feet if danger threatens.

THE PARTNERSHIP BETWEEN HORSE AND HUMANS GOES BACK MORE THAN 6,000 YEARS TO THE STEPPES WHERE HORSES WERE KEPT FOR FOOD AND, BEFORE THE INVENTION OF THE WHEEL, BECAME OUR FIRST MODE OF TRANSPORT.

NEVER KILL A RAVEN

Especially if it lives at the Tower of London, where ravens are protected by royal decree. But all ravens are traditionally afforded respect, for as well as being birds of wit and wisdom their voices are deemed to be deathly omens.

In London, ravens have guarded the Tower for centuries. In response to complaints by the Astronomer Royal, John Flamsteed (1646–1719), that the birds' activities were marring his observations, Charles II ordered their destruction. But to fulfil the prophecy that the absence of ravens would mean the fall of the monarchy, six were saved. Today, as insurance against accident and illness, seven or eight birds are kept.

Ravens mate for life and have been known to live for over 40 years. They are much bigger than crows and have fatter beaks. They are depicted in the prehistoric cave paintings at Lascaux in France. Grip, Barnaby's pet raven in Charles Dickens' novel *Barnaby Rudge*, perfectly expresses the birds' character and chattering voice when he says:

> *Halloa halloa halloa.*
> *What's the matter here!*
> *Keep up your spirits.*
> *Never say die! Bow*
> *wow wow. I'm a devil,*
> *I'm a devil.*

Legendary ravens

Many legends surround the omnivorous raven (*Corvus corax*), the world's largest all-black songbird:

In the Bible, ravens brought food to the wilderness for the prophet Elijah.

The fluttering of ravens above him is said to have warned the Roman orator Cicero of his impending death.

According to the legends of the Pacific Northwest the raven was the creator of the world and bringer of daylight.

In Swedish legend ravens are the ghosts of murdered men.

When the raven croaks, beware. When it says 'Corpse, corpse' people will sicken and die.

The god Thor was said to have kept in touch with the inhabitants of his kingdom through two ravens, called Munin (Memory) and Hugin (Thought).

Ravens can smell death and are associated in history with places of execution where, after observing the proceedings, they would peck at discarded bodies.

THE DEEPER THE CLOUD, THE HARDER IT SHOWERS

This accurate weather forecast is based on the reliable association between heavy rainfall and the appearance of towering cumulonimbus clouds in the sky. When the sun emerges between the clouds and the showers a rainbow may arch across the sky, sometimes in a double bow.

Cumulus clouds are heaped, but cumulonimbus are towering, mountainous ones, named from the Latin *nimbus*, meaning rain. The base is usually dark and the top is either wispy and fibrous, where water is freezing into ice crystals, or flattened into an anvil shape.

Incidentally...

The rainbow, produced when raindrops split white light into its component spectrum of colours, was God's sign to Noah that the flood was over and his people's punishment complete. Although fabled to have a pot of gold at its end, the rainbow is thought by some to be unlucky. Pointing at the rainbow is said to be the surest way of bringing the rain back again.

From clouds of this kind, heavy 'hard' showers may easily develop into full-scale thunderstorms. Cumulonimbus clouds develop only when the air is deeply unstable and mostly in summer when upward air currents are strongest. They form quickly and are usually short-lived. Once they have dropped their payload of rain – or hail or snow – they may quickly peter out. A cumulonimbus cloud with an anvil top is known as a cumulonimbus incus. The largest of these, which are especially common in the tropics, can reach 6 miles (10km) in height – higher than Mount Everest. Ahead of a very severe storm you may see the top of the anvil bulge. This is caused by an updraft of air carrying a parcel of cloud into the stratosphere.

TORNADO ALERT: IF PENDULOUS BREAST-LIKE BLOBS OF CLOUD HANG FROM THE UNDERSIDE OF THE ANVIL (DESCRIBED AS CUMULONIMBUS WITH MAMMATUS) A SEVERE THUNDERSTORM IS IMMINENT, AND POSSIBLY A TORNADO.

ELEPHANTS NEVER FORGET

Close scientific studies of elephant herds prove this to be true. These remarkable creatures are not only able to memorize information essential to their survival but also seem to mourn their dead.

In the elephant family herd, which can number up to 20 females and their young (both male and female), the memory of the senior female, the matriarch, is crucial. It is she who remembers the location of fruitful food sources and reliable waterholes, even those located beneath desiccated mud. She also knows where danger lies, and all the females in the group will clearly remember the distinctive smells of hyenas, lions and other predators.

Incidentally...

*The easiest way to distinguish an African elephant (*Loxodonta africana*) from the Asian elephant (*Elephas maximus*) is that the African species has larger ears and a less humped back.*

Elephant language

Rogue elephant – An aggressive individual living away from the herd.

Pink elephant – A hallucinatory animal seen only by the inebriated.

White elephant – An object of no use other than to give away.

Elephant and Castle – A part of London, but originally the name of a pub deriving from the ancient habit of placing a howdah or 'castle' on the back of a war elephant.

Elephant's foot – An African relative of the yam with a root resembling an elephant's foot.

The result of elephants' powerful memories are 'elephant roads', tracks that often penetrate dense forest and are used for generations. When a matriarch dies a mature female, often her oldest surviving daughter, takes over the leadership and she, too, will remember routes taken regularly since she was a calf.

An elephant herd will often break into smaller groups, especially when food is scarce. On reuniting, the animals greet each other noisily, touching each other with their trunks. When an animal is ill the others in the herd cluster around, trumpeting their distress. If a mother elephant loses her calf she will stay with her dead infant, chasing off predators. And when they encounter the bones of a carcass, elephants will stop to touch them, as if in mourning, and even carry them off into the bushes.

A BUTTERFLY LIVES FOR JUST ONE DAY

An exaggerated claim: without becoming a meal for a bird or bat, and allowed to fulfil its natural span, the minimum lifetime of a butterfly is about a week. But some butterflies, especially those that hibernate or migrate, can live for a year or more.

For a butterfly, food is a major factor in determining lifespan. As a general rule, butterflies that feed solely on nectar – a high sugar but short-lived energy source – live for only two to four weeks. Butterflies of this kind include the papilios, a large group to which the swallowtails belong. Longer-lived butterflies, such as the beautiful heliconids of Central and South America and the clearwings of Costa Rica, which can live for up to 13 months, feed on both nectar and pollen, a diet that provides more sustained energy.

While most die at the end of summer, some butterflies, including the richly coloured peacocks (*Inachis io*) with distinctive 'eyes' on their wings, hibernate over the winter months in sheds and outhouses. On mild winter days they may emerge briefly. If so they should be left alone and discouraged from flying out into the open – to their deaths.

Of all long-lived butterflies, the most remarkable are the orange and black monarchs (*Danaus plexippus*) of the northern USA and southern Canada. The adults that emerge in spring have a lifespan of only a few weeks, but those emerging in autumn migrate by the million to California, Mexico and Florida, where they spend the winter. Their journey time exceeds the lifetime of the spring-born butterflies. On reaching their destinations they cluster in huge groups on 'butterfly trees', which are used year after year (and probably located by smell) by new generations of adults.

After early spring mating at the overwintering sites, the males die and the females head north, then lay their eggs on milkweed before they too die. The caterpillars – an unmistakable green with yellow and white stripes – feed day and night on the milkweed then, like all butterflies, change into chrysalises from which newly metamorphosed adults emerge.

IN THE MID 1960S, AT THE HEIGHT OF HIS PROWESS IN THE RING, THE BOXER MUHAMMAD ALI COINED THE CATCHPHRASE 'FLOAT LIKE A BUTTERFLY, STING LIKE A BEE'.

WHEN THE SCARLET PIMPERNEL CLOSES IT'S GOING TO RAIN

Not for nothing is this small, bright red flower known as the poor man's weatherglass, change-of-the-weather, shepherd's sundial and weather flower. It will invariably close its petals if the sky becomes overcast ahead of rain.

Incidentally...

The Scarlet Pimpernel (Sir Peter Blakeney), the elusive fictional character, created by Baroness Orczy (1865–1947), was named from his use of the little red flower as his emblem.

The scarlet pimpernel (*Anagallis arvensis*), a common weed of gardens, waste ground and dunes, is not, however, an all-day forecaster. For whatever the weather it will have closed its petals by 2 pm and will keep them shut until 8 am. If the petals open fully in the morning a fine day can be expected. But the reverse is not true. When the flowers fail to open first thing it is likely to remain cloudy, but the chance of rainfall is little better than about 15 per cent.

Like the scarlet pimpernel, other flowers, including daisies (*Bellis* spp) and bindweeds (*Convolvulus* spp) close when the day is damp because the cells at the base of the petals detect and respond to increasing levels of moisture in the air. When they close towards the end of the day the petals are responding to lowering levels of sunlight.

The 18th-century Swedish botanist Carolus Linnaeus, known as the father of taxonomy, devised a famous floral timepiece, 'a clock by which one could tell the time, even in cloudy weather, as accurately as by a watch', based on the specific times at which some flowers open and close each day. As he observed, 'The Crepis [hawksbeard] began to open its flowers at 6 a.m. and they were fully open by 6.30. The Leontodon [hawkbit] opened all its flowers between 6 and 7 a.m...' The scarlet pimpernel occupied the eight o'clock position.

A SWARM OF BEES IN MAY IS WORTH A LOAD OF HAY

… A swarm of bees in June is worth a silver spoon. A swarm of bees in July is not worth a fly.' Or in other words, by late summer the value of the swarm is minimal.

Honey bees (*Apis mellifera*) swarm to increase their numbers. In early summer the young queens are ready to fly from the hive, or from wild colonies established in old buildings or hollow trees. At the same time the workers become restless: they gather at the hive entrance, then go back in again to raid the honey cells for food.

When a new queen emerges, about half the workers first cluster, then swarm, around her as she flies off. If the queen has already been impregnated by a drone the swarm will seek a new home. If not, it may return to the hive it has just left, in which case any remaining unfertilized queens will be killed by the worker bees.

Bee myths

No doubt because of their value, bees feature in many other superstitions:

If you dream of bees: you have unknown enemies trying to do you some mischief.

If a swarm settles on the roof of a house or the dead branch of a tree, it is a sign of death.

It is also a sign of death if a swarm comes down the chimney.

Do not drive a bee out of the house: you will drive out good luck.

To keep your bees, and to stop them stinging, inform the bees of a forthcoming wedding – and leave them a piece of cake.

When someone dies, tell the bees and put the hive into mourning with black ribbons; otherwise they too will die and will no longer bring you good luck.

During the summer a colony of honey bees consists of about **50,000** workers (sterile females) a few hundred drones (males) and one queen. The workers make the honey, which sustains them and which they feed to the queen and the drones over the winter. Of the 440lb (200kg) or more of honey that a colony may produce, only about a third is used by the bees themselves. And the better use the swarm makes of the profusion of early summer flowers, the more honey they make.

Ivy can pull a house down

Maybe not literally, but it can do serious damage if it penetrates cracks or crevices in weakened bricks or the mortar between them. Nor will it often kill a tree, though it may weaken one by depriving it of water and nutrients.

The ivy (*Hedera helix*) clings to its support – whether living or not – with 'bearded' stems. The beards are in fact overground or aerial roots, which the plant uses to suck up additional moisture and dissolved minerals. Ivy can be so vigorous that it can grow to the height of a three-storey house or a mature tree, producing its own trunks up to a foot (30cm) across.

As ivy matures the leaves change in shape from triangular to diamond-shaped. It produces its pale green flowers late in the year and even on a sunny winter day you can see it buzzing with hungry insects relishing the energy-packed pollen. Beekeepers have long appreciated the value of ivy in topping up insects' winter supplies of both nectar and pollen.

All about ivy

Ivy has long country associations with health, love and luck:

Ivy leaves will charm away warts and verrucas.

Give ivy to a ewe after birthing to restore her appetite.

Gather ivy and give it to cattle before noon on Christmas Day and the Devil will stay away for a year.

Place an ivy wreath on a grave on All Saint's Day (1 November) to keep a soul safe.

If a girl tucks an ivy leaf down her bosom, the next man who speaks to her will be her own true love.

To cure children of whooping cough, feed them from a bowl made of ivy wood.

The louder the frog, the more the rain

Frogs definitely perk up and 'sing' more forcefully when the air is damp, whether or not rain is on the way. It is the males that have the loud voices – they employ them in the mating season to attract a female partner.

Incidentally...

The edible European frog most favoured by French gastronomes is Rana esculenta. *According to the renowned French chef Auguste Escoffier (1846–1935) they are best poached in white wine, then steeped in a fish sauce with paprika and finally set into champagne jelly 'to counterfeit the effect of water'. Preceding this last stage, Escoffier recommended arranging sprigs of chervil and tarragon between the legs to resemble grass.*

It is a truth of amphibian life that a moist skin is essential for activity, which is why, when on land, frogs prefer being in damp places. The frog's croak, used to attract a fertile female, reaches a loud boom in the bullfrog (*Rana catesbeina*), whose voice is amplified by large resonating sacs at the side of its throat. By contrast, the common frog (*R. temporaria*), widespread in Europe, has a deep, rasping croak. The females reply with softer chirrups and grunts.

Frogs are good for the garden: as well as insects they consume large quantities of slugs and snails (shells included) as well as insects of all kinds. Flying insects are caught on the sticky tip of the long tongue, which is attached at the front of the mouth and quickly thrust out towards passing prey.

IN COUNTRY DISTRICTS, PARENTS WOULD BRIEFLY PUT A LIVE FROG INTO THE MOUTH OF A CHILD SUFFERING FROM AN INFECTION OF THRUSH, IN THE EXPECTATION OF A CURE. A BLACK RIBBON, PULLED THROUGH THE BODY OF A LIVE FROG AND TIED AROUND THE NECK OF A SUFFERER, WAS USED TO CURE WHOOPING COUGH.

THROW OUT A SPRAT TO CATCH A MACKEREL

In other words, use a small bait to catch a bigger fish, or do someone a small favour in the hope of a handsome return. In reality, just a hook, line and a lure – or live bait – is all you need to catch these tasty fish.

The prolific Atlantic mackerel (*Scomber scomber*), which was for centuries an important food in both Europe and North America, lives in shoals up to 10,000 strong from northern Labrador to the North African coast. It feeds

Incidentally...

A mackerel sky is a cloud formation of wavy stripes created by globular altocumulus clouds, which look like the iridescent blue-green lines on the side of the Atlantic mackerel. 'Mackerel sky/Never long wet, never long dry' is one of the more reliable predictions among traditional weather lore.

mostly on plankton, krill, fish eggs and small fish – including sprats. It is a spectacular sight at night to see mackerel 'firing' upwards through schools of micro-organisms which, as they are disturbed, give off luminescent flashes.

Catching mackerel from a small boat offshore can be highly rewarding and the fish, cooked on the beach within minutes of landing, have an incomparably fresh taste. In open seas a mackerel can swim at up to 20 miles (32km) an hour, fast enough to evade its many swift enemies such as tuna, porpoises and swordfish. A single hook decorated with red feathers and plastic spheres can attract eight or more fish at one dip of the line.

Sprats (*Sprattus sprattus*) are a distinct species belonging to the herring family, not just small herrings (*Clupea harengus*). Though small, they are good to eat. In London, Lord Mayor's Day, 9 November, was once known as Sprat Day because it was the official start of the sprat-eating season.

> The biggest Atlantic mackerel ever caught on a rod – in deep water off the western coast of Sweden in 1995 – weighed 6lb 12oz (3.074kg).

THE FOX MAY GROW GREY, BUT NEVER GOOD

This saying epitomizes the cunning of the fox and its reputation as a wily hunter that does not change it ways, even with age. It features in folklore from around the world as a cunning trickster.

The face of the fox (*Vulpes vulpes*), with its pointed, slender nose – equipped with an acute sense of smell – sharp eyes and pricked ears, is the picture of cleverness. But its penchant for poultry, and its instinct for killing more birds than it could ever eat, makes this wily

Incidentally...

The fox wraps itself in its bushy tail, or brush, to keep warm at night. For women, wearing a fox fur around the neck – complete with the head, and often with jewels in place of the eyes – was the height of 1930s fashion.

animal the farmer's enemy. It is rumoured
that a fox will carry off a goose from the
farmyard with the head in its mouth and the
body slung over its shoulder.

Though long and vigorously hunted as
a pest and for sport, the fox continues to
thrive in both country and town through its
adaptability, opportunism and cunning.
When chased by hounds, foxes will dive into
one of many 'earths', backtrack on their own
trails, walk along the tops of fences and even
run through flocks of sheep.

In towns, foxes thrive anywhere food is
on tap from rubbish bags or dustbins (they
push the lids off with their noses), and will
make earths for breeding and raising cubs in
secluded spots in parks and gardens. If you
catch an animal's eyes in your headlights and
they shine white or blue then you've most
probably encountered a fox. A cat's eyes glow
greenish yellow.

In American folklore, the
trickster fox was popularized
as Brer Fox in the *Uncle
Remus* tales by Joel Chandler
Harris (1848–1908).
Based on both European
and African–American
traditions, he is out-classed
in wit and wiliness by his
companion Brer Rabbit.

ACCORDING TO FOLKLORE,
A FOX GETS RID OF FLEAS
IN ITS FUR BY TAKING A
LEAF IN ITS MOUTH THEN
WALKING BACKWARDS INTO
WATER UNTIL IT IS ENTIRELY
SUBMERGED, MAKING THE
FLEAS EITHER MOVE ON TO
THE LEAF OR BE DROWNED.

CATS ALWAYS FALL ON THEIR FEET

Remarkably, they do. Using a combination of instinctive reactions and rapid movements they can right themselves in seconds, adding to their legendary abilities to survive danger.

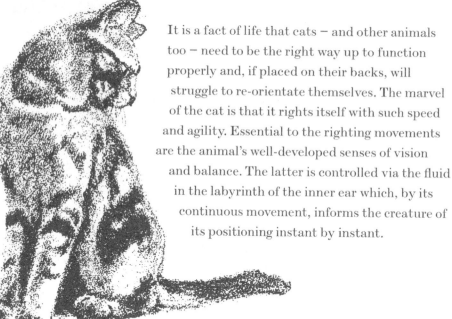

It is a fact of life that cats – and other animals too – need to be the right way up to function properly and, if placed on their backs, will struggle to re-orientate themselves. The marvel of the cat is that it rights itself with such speed and agility. Essential to the righting movements are the animal's well-developed senses of vision and balance. The latter is controlled via the fluid in the labyrinth of the inner ear which, by its continuous movement, informs the creature of its positioning instant by instant.

Incidentally ...

The idea that cats have nine lives – one less it is said, than a woman – comes from their proverbial skill at surviving disaster. Cats have been known to emerge, unscathed, from homes demolished by bombs or earthquakes.

Slow-motion filming confirms that a falling cat performs a set sequence of movements. First the body is bent from the 'waist' at an angle of 90°, with the front limbs kept close to the head and the hind legs splayed out from the trunk. Next the front part of the body is rotated through 180°, bringing the forelimbs vertical to the ground. Finally the back part of the body is rotated and the cat is the right way up with legs extended, ready for a perfect landing.

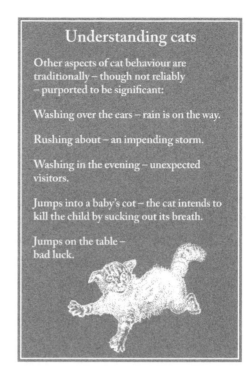

Understanding cats

Other aspects of cat behaviour are traditionally – though not reliably – purported to be significant:

Washing over the ears – rain is on the way.

Rushing about – an impending storm.

Washing in the evening – unexpected visitors.

Jumps into a baby's cot – the cat intends to kill the child by sucking out its breath.

Jumps on the table – bad luck.

MOTHS COME OUT ONLY AT NIGHT

Most moths are nocturnal – but by no means all. Luckily for the enthusiast many day-flying moths are superbly coloured, their bright hues often advertising to birds the fact that they are poisonous.

Of all the world's day-flying moths one of the most spectacular is the humming-bird hawk-moth (*Macroglossum stellatarum*). The moth, common in eastern

Incidentally...

Attracted by the light, moths will often come indoors on summer nights. According to a country tradition, if a moth flies once around the light a postcard is on the way, twice a letter and three times a parcel.

Asia and across southern Europe, reaches southern Britain in large numbers in warm summers. Just like its avian namesake it hovers over flowers, sipping nectar from blooms such as phloxes and verbenas with its long proboscis and darting from one flower to the next. If your hearing is acute enough you may also be able to detect the high-pitched noise of its wing beats.

Night-flying moths are mostly drab in colour and, though inconspicuous (many look very like leaves), can often be seen on vegetation during daylight hours. They use their powerful sense of smell to locate nectar. Unlike butterflies, which usually hold their wings together at 90° to their bodies, most moths lay their wings out flat when at rest. Look too, for the feathery moth antennae, compared with the knob-tipped antennae of butterflies.

The day-flying five-spot burnet moth (*Zygaena trifolii*), whose grey wings are splashed with scarlet, is a species that birds learn to avoid. The moths' bodies contain cyanide, which is formed from food by the caterpillars and transmitted to the adult during metamorphosis.

THE CATERPILLARS OF THE ISABELLA TIGER MOTH (*PYRRHARCTIA ISABELLA*) ARE CALLED WOOLLY BEARS BECAUSE THEY ARE SMALL, DARK AND COVERED IN BRISTLES.

WHEN YOU CAN TREAD ON NINE DAISIES AT ONCE, SPRING HAS COME

O r three, or a dozen. The saying varies from family to family. These pretty 'earthbound stars' as the poet Chaucer called them, can be seen in flower nearly all year but burst into a profusion of blooms in April and May.

The daisy is named in two ways. The common name comes from 'day's eye', referring to the fact that it opens at dawn to reveal a flower with a miniature sun at its centre and closes its pink-tinged petals at sunset. Its generic name *Bellis* comes from the Latin for beautiful – its specific epithet *perennis* refers, botanically, to its perennial nature.

Daisies, though no longer part of the herbalist's armoury, once had a variety of uses in medicine. John Gerard recommended sniffing the juice of the roots and leaves up the nostrils to 'purge' the head. For the lovesick, alternate picking of petals while chanting 'He loves me, he loves me not' until only one is left is an old form of relaxation therapy.

Incidentally...

In cricket, a daisy-cutter is a ball that reaches the batsman rolling along the ground. It is named from the fact that the plant's rosette of leaves lies flat to the ground – where it is also beyond the reach of mower blades.

INDEX

Page numbers in **bold** refer to sayings